STUDIES IN ECONOMIC AND SOCIAL HISTORY

This series, specially commissioned by the Economic History Society, provides a guide to the current interpretations of the key themes of economic and social history in which advances have recently been made or in which there has been significant debate.

Originally entitled 'Studies in Economic History', in 1974 the series had its scope extended to include topics in social history, and the new series title, 'Studies in Economic and Social History', signalises this development.

The series gives readers access to the best work done, helps them to draw their own conclusions in major fields of study, and by means of the critical bibliography in each book guides them in the selection of further reading. The aim is to provide a spring-board to further work rather than a set of pre-packaged conclusions or short-cuts.

ECONOMIC HISTORY SOCIETY

The Economic History Society, which numbers over 3000 members, publishes the *Economic History Review* four times a year (free to members) and holds an annual conference. Enquiries about membership should be addressed to the Assistant Secretary, Economic History Society, Peterhouse, Cambridge. Fulltime students may join the Society at special rates.

STUDIES IN ECONOMIC AND SOCIAL HISTORY

Edited for the Economic History Society by L. A. Clarkson

PUBLISHED

OTHER TITLES ARE IN PREPARATION

Approaches to the History of the Western Family, 1500–1914

Prepared for
The Economic History Society by

MICHAEL ANDERSON

Professor of Economic History,
University of Edinburgh

MACMILLAN

© The Economic History Society 1980

First published 1980
Reprinted 1984, 1985, 1986

Published by
MACMILLAN EDUCATION LTD
Houndmills, Basingstoke, Hampshire RG21 2XS
and London
Companies and representatives
throughout the world

Printed in Hong Kong

British Library Cataloguing in Publication Data
Anderson, Michael, b. 1942
Approaches to the history of the Western family
1500-1914. - (Studies in economic and social history).
1. Family - History
I. Title   II. Series
301.42'1'091812   HQ515
ISBN 0-333-24065-0

Contents

Acknowledgements

I have benefited greatly from comments and suggestions made by Christopher Smout, Elspeth Moodie and Ann-Sofie Kälvemark. My current and past students will also recognise arguments worked through in discussion with them. As always the members of the Cambridge Group for the History of Population and Social Structure have been generous in providing information on work in progress and in providing access to references and material of which I was unaware.

Note on References

References in the text within square brackets relate to the numbered items in the Select Bibliography, followed, where necessary, by the page numbers in italics, for example [1:45].

Editor's Preface

SINCE 1968, when the Economic History Society and Macmillan published the first of the 'Studies in Economic and Social History', the series has established itself as a major teaching tool in universities, colleges and schools, and as a familiar landmark in serious bookshops throughout the country. A great deal of the credit for this must go to the wise leadership of its first editor, Professor M. W. Flinn, who retired at the end of 1977. The books tend to be bigger now than they were originally, and inevitably more expensive; but they have continued to provide information in modest compass at a reasonable price by the standards of modern academic publication.

There is no intention of departing from the principles of the first decade. Each book aims to survey findings and discussion in an important field of economic or social history that has been the subject of recent lively debate. It is meant as an introduction for readers who are not themselves professional researchers but who want to know what the discussion is all about – students, teachers and others generally interested in the subject. The authors, rather than either taking a strongly partisan line or suppressing their own critical faculties, set out the arguments and the problems as fairly as they can, and attempt a critical summary and explanation of them from their own judgement. The discipline now embraces so wide a field in the study of the human past that it would be inappropriate for each book to follow an identical plan, but all volumes will normally contain an extensive descriptive bibliography.

The series is not meant to provide all the answers but to help readers to see the problems clearly enough to form their own conclusions. We shall never agree in history, but

9

the discipline will be well served if we know what we are disagreeing about, and why.

University of St Andrews   *Editor*

1 Introduction

MY aim in this pamphlet is to provide a guide for those who wish to explore the burgeoning literature on the history of the Western family since the sixteenth century. Over the past twenty years family history has been one of the main growth areas in the development of social history; indeed, little of the literature discussed in this pamphlet was written before 1960 and most was published after 1970. On the one hand the newness has made family history immensely exciting – so much has had to be discovered and many of the discoveries have been so unexpected. On the other hand there have been difficulties. As in any pioneering discipline some lines of inquiry have proved totally fruitless. The many hours of detailed work necessary to produce results for even a single community have meant that progress has been slow. The fact that most work has been based on single villages or small regions has made it extraordinarily difficult to build up a clear picture of the main changes in family life over the past 400 years. Indeed, as we shall see, there are still major disputes even over which questions should be asked.

Almost inevitably in all this activity, controversy and disagreement between scholars favouring different ways forward have been common; some of the attacks made on other people's research have by normal academic standards been quite abusive, with scholars implying that their opponents' work was either irrelevant or almost totally lacking in scholarly judgement and rigour. Superficially – and as occurs in any area of history – these disagreements have often seemed to be over the interpretation of particular sets of documents or the significance to be attached to particular events. And, in part, this has been so. But the disagreements can also be traced to two other sources.

Firstly, there is the problem of diversity – indeed, the one unambiguous fact which has emerged in the last twenty years is that there can be no simple history of *the* Western family since the sixteenth century because there is not, nor ever has there been, a single family system. The West has always been characterised by diversity of family forms, by diversity of family functions and by diversity in attitudes to family relationships not only over time but at any one point in time. There is, except at the most trivial level, no Western family type. Peasant families have typically differed markedly from merchant families and labouring families from aristocratic families. Peasants in eighteenth-century north-west France differed from peasants in central France, and in Germany or Sweden marked differences could be found even between neighbouring communities. England perhaps alone appears to have been much more homogenous yet even here illegitimacy in one area could occur twice as frequently as in another. Everywhere, certain groups – large like French Canadians or small like Hutterite communities – had behaviour which differed markedly from the rest of the society in which they lived and one group, North-American black families, have been the subject of so much controversy that I have been unable to include a discussion of the topic here. For the same reason I have excluded discussion of the very limited literature on the dramatic changes which have occurred since the inter-war period; indeed, the history of the Western family since the end of the First World War has been remarkably neglected, as is, of course, the case with so many other areas of social history.

Identifying and trying to understand the diversity has been a major problem, particularly in any attempt to generalise about long-run trends over the Western world as a whole. Many scholars, however, have set out to do just this, hence the necessity for this pamphlet to have a wide geographical focus and a long temporal span. But underlying these difficulties lies a second and much more fundamental set of issues, which in fact arise in any area of economic and social history – and indeed in any area of social science – but which are seldom as clear as they have

14

been in family history. It has been becoming increasingly clear in recent years that many of the disputes in family history arise because different groups of scholars, even when apparently working on the same topic, are, often unconsciously, trying to write very different kinds of history and are thus adopting different approaches to the selection of problems for research, to the kinds of sources they employ, to the way evidence is and can be used, and to the relevance of social and economic theory to their work.

I have here distinguished four different approaches to family history. One, which calls itself psychohistory and even has its own journal, the *Journal of Psychohistory*, seems already in its work on the family to have run into insoluble problems of evidence, and to have involved its practitioners in so much anachronistic judgement and blatant disregard for many of the basic principles of historical scholarship, that I have not thought it worth detailed consideration here; a summary of the main lines of approach of this school together with a useful collection of critiques can be found in the first number of the *History of Childhood Quarterly* (see also [54] and Wishy's review in *Journal of Family History*, 1978). The remaining three approaches – which I here call the demographic, the sentiments and the household economics approaches – continue to attract much attention and I have devoted a chapter to each. I shall argue, indeed, that each represents one major tradition of social science writing, that each has its own significant and individual contribution to make to our understanding of family life in the past and that the pursuit of all three is necessary if a properly rounded and sensitive picture is to be obtained; in fact, as we shall see few scholars stay totally within one tradition, and the distinctions between approaches, while they reflect clear differences in emphasis between different scholars, are to some extent oversimplifications.

Though the subject is of immense intrinsic interest, because problems of methodology are so important, students will not always find the study of this subject simple. The evidence, indeed, often appears fragmented and confusing, and the analysis ambiguous. However, because of the light that it throws on current approaches to social history in general, a careful examination of how modern historians are treating family history is particularly illuminating at the present time.

2 The Demographic Approach

BEFORE the mid-1950s family history as we know it today was almost nonexistent. Most work was limited to single families or small élite groups or was based mainly on impressionistic literary sources. Very little was known about the family life of the mass of the population.

Then, in the mid-1950s a group of demographers in France greatly refined (and extended to the populations of whole communities) the old technique of using the parish registers of baptisms, burials and marriages to link together the entries which related to the same individual and family (a useful introduction to this work by Goubert is in [11]). The findings derived from this 'family reconstitution' – and notably the demonstration of the use of some form of conscious family limitation among the Genevan bourgeoisie as early as the seventeenth century – caused other scholars to take up their methods and to extend this demographic approach to other sources of data. It is this body of work which is reviewed in this chapter.

The basic principles which inform this approach have their inspiration in the methods of natural science and of quantitative social science. The pioneering work of the Cambridge Group for the History of Population and Social Structure, for example, has been particularly concerned with the development of rigorous, standardised and quantitative research procedures aimed at generating data comparable both over long periods of time and across communities and societies. The literary sources which formed the basis of most earlier attempts at family history are largely rejected on the grounds that their evidence is difficult to interpret reliably, often contradictory and above all uncertain in its relevance outside a small élite.

Instead, those who have worked in this tradition have

17

turned their attention to sources – particularly parish registers on the one hand and census-type listings created for
taxation and other purposes on the other – which cover the
entire populations of at least some communities. While this
has limited the range of topics that they can cover, on these
topics they have built up huge data banks of internationally
comparable data covering long periods of time. In doing so
they have shown the falsity of many traditional views about
the past, and have set up a solid base of data on which all
family historians today rely as a framework for their
analysis. Let us consider some examples.

(i) MARRIAGE RATES AND AGES

From 1600 until the late nineteenth century – and probably
back into medieval times – Western Europe had a marriage
pattern almost unique in world history [31]. For example,
marriage was late. Typical mean ages of marriage in rural
areas were 27 or 28 for men and 25 or 26 for women, and
between 1600 and 1850 there is little evidence of any
systematic or long-run patterns of change [29; 28] (though
Wrigley has recently suggested a rise in England in the age
for women until about 1700 followed by a fall to a low point
in the mid-nineteenth century, but with no similar pattern
for men [30]). After 1850 some rise is detectable in a
number of countries and as late as the 1930s the mean age
at first marriage for women in England and Wales was still
25 and that for men 27 (compared with 22 and 24 in the
1970s). Before 1850 only in North America were younger
ages of marriage normal for whole populations and even
these were significantly above present-day levels in most
places. Moreover, significant proportions of the population
never married. Before 1800 typical proportions were
around 10 per cent though in some areas in the later
nineteenth century figures nearer or even in excess of 20
per cent can be found; again, only in the last 30 years have
these rates changed dramatically.

But these are mean figures and can be misleading. Both
between communities and even in the same place over time
there were significant variations: for example, in Shepshed
in the English midlands the mean age of marriage fell

between the sixteenth and the early nineteenth centuries by over five years for both sexes [74]. However, it is one thing to find differences of this kind and quite another to explain them; and at least before the nineteenth century very little success has been achieved here, partly because much of the variation is probably the result of random variation brought about by the small size of the communities studied (a general problem of all demographic work on individual pre-industrial communities) and partly because demographic theory has not been greatly concerned with nuptiality. The main problem is, however, as we shall see, that the emphasis of research has been mainly on description rather than analysis and that the research has been done in ways which make it unlikely that easily verifiable interpretations will emerge.

(ii) PATTERNS OF CHILDBEARING

A detailed account of the literature on marital fertility is outside the scope of this pamphlet and a number of useful discussions appear elsewhere [21; 22; 23; Tilly in 18]. As with the literature on marriage, more effort has so far gone into description than into analysis and the diverse findings are poorly integrated. However, a number of points are fairly clear.

Before the late nineteenth century (except in France where changes came earlier), a combination of a late age of marriage and relatively long birth intervals gave mean completed family sizes (number of children born per woman) for most areas of between 5 and 6.5 (though with wide dispersal about the means). In some areas, and for certain groups of the population as early as the seventeenth century, some form of family limitation of a conscious and active kind seems to have been employed, keeping completed family size down below 5 for significant periods of time [25; 26]. Whether or not family size rose in the eighteenth century is an open question but recent evidence suggests a small rise (a full description for England will appear in [23]). What is certain is that, by the late eighteenth century in France and possibly, though the figures have to be inferred from poor data, in North America (summarised by Withey in *J. Fam. Hist.* 1978) and by the later nineteenth century elsewhere, a sustained decline was under way which was of crucial importance in making possible new attitudes and experiences within the Western family [7; 24]. In England and Wales, for example, completed family size fell from about 6 in the marriage cohort of 1860–70 to about 4 for the 1900 cohort and 3 by that of 1910.

For the family historian, however, it is not so much the reduced number of children as their changed distribution over the marital life cycle which is of most significance. In pre-twentieth-century populations births were spread fairly evenly over the whole fertile period with only a small fall as women aged. By contrast, since 1900 the main effect of fertility limitation has been to compress childbearing into the early years of married life so that, compared with a mean period from first marriage to last child for seventeenth- and eighteenth-century European populations of 14.4 years [28] and a median period of 11.5 years for American wives born 1880–9, the figure for those born in the 1950s will be less than 8.5 [33; note also Wells in 11]. Since, over the same period, the age of marriage has also fallen, the age at which women had their last child fell even more from a mean of 40.1 before 1800 [28] to 33 for wives born in the 1880s and 30 for those born in the 1920s. Together with falling adult mortality, the consequence has been that whereas a woman who marries in the late twentieth century at the mean age of marriage can expect to live for almost 50 years after the birth of her last child [32], women marrying before the late nineteenth century could expect to live only for about 20 years, a figure that showed little change over time. Looking in a different way, the mean duration of a marriage unbroken by divorce has risen from about 20 years (with a wide local dispersal) in pre-industrial Europe to about 35 by 1900 and to at least 45 years today. Only couples born in the last 100 years have been able to look forward as a matter of course to a period of old age together free from the cares of bringing up children. (The changed familial and economic position of women as a result of these changes is usefully summarised in [90: *ch. 5*].)

(iii) EXTRAMARITAL CONCEPTIONS

The history of extramarital conceptions since the early eighteenth century falls into three distinct phases which show a remarkable parallelism across the whole Western world. Firstly, almost everywhere, the eighteenth and early nineteenth centuries were periods of steady rise in both illegitimate births and prenuptial conceptions, though the scale and timing of the start of the rise varied from country to country and region to region. Secondly, at some point in the nineteenth century (though not until the 1930s in Sweden) this general rise in illegitimacy was halted and the trends, with some inter-country variation, went into reverse, a fall which continued slowly until the Second World War (usefully summarised in [41]). The data on premarital pregnancy are less complete; it certainly fell in England and Wales over this period but in North America, for example, an early-nineteenth-century fall seems to have been followed by a late-nineteenth-century rise [45]. The third phase in European non-marital conception belongs to the post-war period and took the form of a dramatic rise which in some places is still continuing.

These three major phases are well documented for a range of countries and form one of the most impressive and interesting bodies of data collected within the demographic approach (and there is now some evidence of even earlier internationally parallel trends, notably a fall in the first part of the seventeenth century [1; 7]). But around these parallel trends there were also significant variations. Even within the same country some areas had figures three or four times as high as others though the reasons are often debatable ([46] for Scotland [1] for England [41] for Europe generally and Kälvemark in [40] for Sweden). Significant variations also occurred by social class, a pattern which also changed over time. At least in France bastard-bearing seems to have been widely spread through the population in the sixteenth century [7; Depauw in 12]. In later periods a largely working-class pattern has been observed which also seems to have applied to prenuptial conception, though not necessarily in some peasant areas (there is good work here on North America – see [45]). More recently there has been a return to a more equal distribution through the population. And the distribution of illegitimate births across the population seems to have changed in a third way too. Several English and French studies, for the pre-nineteenth-century period in particular, suggest that part of the fluctuation in illegitimacy rates was the result of variation in the behaviour of what Laslett has called a 'subsociety of bastard bearers', women who bore more than one illegitimate child [1; 40]. (A tendency for the 'inheritance' of prenuptial pregnancy between generations has also been noted.) Just who these women were is not as yet clear, but if further research can substantiate and locate more precisely the existence of such a subsociety an important set of clues as to the sources of variation in extramarital sexual behaviour over time may be obtained.

One other observation is also apposite here. The correlation between the fluctuations in illegitimacy and those of prenuptial conceptions has already been noted (and this, of course, rules out any simple explanation that fluctuations in illegitimacy result from changes in the pressures on unmarried pregnant girls to get married). More interestingly, though more tentatively, a rough parallel has also been noted between illegitimate and legitimate fertility – both probably rose in the eighteenth century, fell at the end of the nineteenth and rose in the post-war era. Similarly there is an inverse correlation with the age of marriage, at least in England and Wales, and particularly in the eighteenth century. Certainly there is no evidence for any period to support the superficially attractive proposition that illegitimacy has been high when women have had to wait longer to get married and been lower when marriage was earlier.

(iv) SIZE AND MEMBERSHIP OF THE HOUSEHOLD

There can be little doubt that popular tradition in most Western societies has held that households in pre-industrial Europe were relatively large and complex in structure, frequently containing members of more than two successive generations and often including extra kin such as cousins, nieces and nephews, and uncles and aunts (compare, for example, the tradition of the *Ganze Hauz* in Germany, the *storfamilj* in Sweden and the large family community in France). A similar notion had long held credence in academic circles where the most cited authority was one of the founders of modern empirical social science, Frédéric LePlay. LePlay, writing in the second half of the nineteenth century, described three ideal familial types:

(i) the patriarchal (characteristic of nomadic and herding societies), which laid strong emphasis on stability, authority, lineage and tradition, leading to a large domestic group containing at least all the male descendants of the patriarch;

(ii) the stem family, or *famille souche* (widespread, according to LePlay, in European peasant societies), which also had a stable patriarchal element but usually restricted co-residence and succession to one son of the patriarch and his descendants, though some other children might remain unmarried in the household, leading to household sizes of up to 18 persons;

(iii) the unstable family, which characterised urban manufacturing populations and, by contrast with the other types, was founded by the marriage of two independent individuals, survived only as long as they did, and despatched its children into the world as soon as they could be independent, exercising little control over them.

From the mid-1960s Peter Laslett in particular began to accumulate evidence which suggested that, at least in England, large and complex households had never been common. In 1969 Laslett published his first analysis of listings for 100 English communities at dates between 1574 and 1821 and he called a meeting in Cambridge to discuss similar data for other periods and countries (the papers – including Laslett's – are reproduced in [34]). In his paper Laslett demonstrated that the mean household size in England (including servants) had remained more or less constant at about 4.75 from the sixteenth century right through the industrialisation period until the end of the nineteenth century when a steady decline set in to a figure of about 3 in contemporary censuses. Equally remarkable, he suggested, was the small range of the means across the 100 communities. The largest figure was 7.22 (6.63 if London is excluded) while the smallest was 3.63. No obvious pattern of temporal or regional variation could be observed. Only 2 per cent of the households contained 12 or more people and only one-third contained 6 or more. However – and this is an important point which has often been overlooked in the subsequent controversy – Laslett was at pains to point out that a majority of the population (53 per cent) actually lived in households of 6 or more members; a majority of people could live in largish households even if mean household size was small. The full significance of this point is explored below.

This evidence suggested strongly to Laslett that the stem family had not been common in pre-industrial England. Equally, the evidence on household composition seemed to confirm this view. Only 10 per cent of households in the 61 pre-1821 English communities on which relatively reliable data could be obtained had residents who could be identified as kin from beyond the conjugal family of husband, wife and children, these kin making up only 3 per cent of the population. Although 70 per cent of households were classed as two-generational and 24 per cent as one, only 6 per cent contained relatives of three different generations and less than 1 per cent of four. Again no regional or time patterns could be identified in the data though subsequent research has shown that by the mid-nineteenth century the figure for complex households had risen to between 15 and 20 per cent (with, interestingly, particularly high figures being found in industrialised textile towns) [1; 75].

The evidence from other parts of the world produced at the Cambridge conference raised in Laslett's mind an even more interesting proposition, that the stem-family form had never been an important feature of Western European or North American society. As late as 1972 almost nowhere in the pre-industrial literate world was there good quality evidence which showed any significant number of large households and no area of the Western world had been found with more than one quarter of the households containing relatives outside the conjugal family. Indeed

24

Laslett has concluded [1] that a nuclear familial form may have been one of the enduring and fundamental characteristics of the Western family system and thus to be set alongside the European marriage pattern discussed above. He therefore argued that a belief in the stem family has survived only as an act of faith bolstered by what he has called its 'privileged' position in Western social science [20].

Before turning to a discussion of the controversy raised by this proposition let us turn attention to some other findings which emerged as by-products of household analysis. For example, while kin were not common as secondary members of households in the past, non-relatives of various kinds were. In pre-industrial European listings from places other than towns, most of these individuals were described as servants, though from an early date in parts of Europe [67] and in North America individuals described as boarders and lodgers appeared in large numbers in rural areas (as they did in the towns throughout the Western world) [39]. In Laslett's 100 pre-1821 communities, for example, 29 per cent of households contained one or more servants, and servants comprised 13 per cent of the population [34]. Figures in excess of 20 per cent of households and ranging up to over 50 per cent have subsequently been reported for rural communities in many other areas of Europe and North America right through to the end of the nineteenth century. These rural servants were distributed roughly equally between the sexes and were predominantly young (typically two-thirds aged under 25 and at least one-third under 20) and almost all were unmarried (except in parts of Scandinavia where older married servants appear to have been not uncommon). Many of these servants – at least in England and Denmark and possibly slightly less so elsewhere – left home in their early teens and would then have spent 10 to 15 years in service, often changing employer every year and providing most of the non-familial labour force for the farm and artisan households in which they lived. While fewer very young children were involved than was once thought, the importance of this kind of service as a feature of the life experience of a

25

majority of young adults in pre-industrial England remains considerable [34; 60; Netting in *J. Fam. Hist.* 1979].

In urban areas servants were also important, at least until after 1900 (in London in the early eighteenth century one estimate suggests that nearly 60 per cent of households contained servants [38]). However, urban areas also from an early period had large numbers of 'lodgers' and 'boarders'. For example, in Leyden in 1581 4 per cent of the population were lodgers and in London in the 1690s the figure may have been as high as 20 per cent [1:*45*]. Towns in the nineteenth century in both England and North America seem generally to have had at least 15 to 20 per cent of households with co-resident lodgers or boarders (useful general discussions of the topic are in [39; 76]). Typically such lodgers were, like servants, young, single and in small groups of one to three per household, though a substantial minority of conjugal families (usually in the first stages of the family life cycle) were also present. To some extent, leaving home to go into service, setting up in lodgings, living with kin, and continuing to live at home with parents can be seen as alternatives for young people in the early stages of the life cycle. One of the problems for future research is to try to discern who 'chose' which option and why. Clearly the availability of large amounts of wage-labour employment near to home is one factor. In general in both England and North America it seems that industrial urban areas offered to children greater opportunities to continue to live with parents than had been available in domestically organised rural societies [75; 76]. Equally, areas with large migrant populations had large numbers of lodgers, presumably in part because there were fewer kin with whom to live. And shortages of housing, family size and lack of previous cultural aversion to overcrowding were all probably important.

Research on the period since 1850 has charted the steady decline of both lodging and service (servants may already have been in decline in England before 1800 [38]) and the emergence of a new modern pattern in which familial residence is the norm for the young until either marriage or higher education or a well-established career moves them from home [Modell *et al.* in 19]. Already by 1850 male living-in servants, never important in urban areas, had declined in English agriculture except in a few areas and living-in apprenticeship lessened in importance as it was not adopted by the new factory-based industries. Female domestic service, however, remained the largest single occupation for women in Britain until after 1900, large numbers still leaving home at an early age in many other areas of Europe at the same date [1]; only two world wars saw the near extinction of service. Lodging, too, declined markedly in the first fifty years of the present century, in this case aided in North America at least by pressure from moral reformers [39]. As a result of these and other changes (notably the declining age of marriage and the gradual spread and extension of compulsory education) the whole pattern of transition to adulthood has been transformed over the past 100 years with a significant compression in the number of years over which most individuals enter work, marry and establish their own households; along with this has gone a tendency for all these events to occur rather earlier than in the nineteenth century (Modell *et al.* in [19]; Modell *et al.* in *J. Fam. Hist.* 1976). The full implications of these changes for the nature and quality of parent-child relations have yet to be adequately explored.

(v) CRITIQUE OF THE DEMOGRAPHIC APPROACH

Perhaps not surprisingly Laslett's rejection of a long-held popular and academic tradition set off a major controversy which has subsequently extended to a wider attack on the philosophy and methodology of the demographic approach to family history. These criticisms may be considered under five sub-headings.

(a) *The Quality of the Data*

Serious difficulties of both interpretation and comparability arise with most of the pre-census listings and even with the earlier census returns. The listings were usually prepared for administrative purposes like taxation or military recruitment, so that it is often not known whether the listing was even intended to be comprehensive nor precisely what any subdivisions in the listing may mean. This remains a problem even with early censuses; for earlier periods very sweeping assumptions about what the listings mean have to be made and the assumptions become increasingly shaky as comparisons are made between centuries and between societies. Indeed, these difficulties of source interpretation raise major questions concerning the validity and even the internal consistency of some of the comparative exercises which have been attempted using household listings alone (compare Berkner [35] on Laslett [34]; Laslett [20] on Berkner [67]; Anderson in [16]). This point is worth bearing in mind when the efforts of the household economics school (who rely heavily on a comparative method) are being discussed in chapter 4.

Nor is it only in household listings that problems of data quality arise. Most of the data on births and marriages discussed above are derived from family reconstitution. But family reconstitution is only useful in as far as the parish registers are reasonably complete – and there is a major debate over this point (Razzell in *Pop. Studies* 1972; Wrigley in *Pop. Studies* 1975) – and also in as far as what is known as the 'reconstitutable minority' (usually less than a third of all marriages) is representative of the whole population. The problem of small numbers being available for proper analysis is a result of the high rates of population mobility. A similar problem arises when attempts are made to make household analysis more dynamic by linking censuses, a mode of analysis which has become increasingly important among North-American scholars who have laid great stress on the impact on later family behaviour of particular historical events occurring at earlier points in the life cycle (for example [17]; Elder in [19]); but wherever linkages are made the implicit assumption that the non-migrants are representative of the population as a whole is clearly open to question (indeed research on Sweden has already demonstrated significant differences between the behaviour of migrants and non-migrants [Kälvemark in 16; 83]).

(b) *The Atypicality of England*

Laslett's original speculations on household composition were almost entirely derived from English data and it remains true that England is the only country on which a large body of household-listing evidence has been analysed in any systematic fashion. Subsequently, a number of scholars (for example [37; 7; 35]) have attacked Laslett both for basing his argument on inadequate data which ignored the inter-regional variability which was so characteristic of pre-industrial Europe and, in effect, for trying to kill the stem-family hypothesis without looking in those areas of Europe (parts of Germany, Austria, north Italy, north Spain and, above all, southern France) where LePlay had posited its existence. Recent research has produced evidence from a considerable number of communities in central and southern France and in Tuscany where between 20 and 74 per cent of the households were of a complex type; a body of parallel data now also exists on parts of Germany (and on parts of Hungary, Austria, Latvia and Estonia as well as Russia where Laslett had always expected that a different pattern would be found). More unexpected, perhaps, are the substantial numbers of complex households found in some parts of eighteenth-century Sweden [61].

Thus, superficially at least, it seems that the European pre-industrial rural-household pattern was a regionally diverse one with England, northern France, North America and possibly the Low Countries (areas not mentioned by LePlay) being unique in both their low proportions of complex households and their overall homogeneity of household patterns. By contrast, areas of much greater complexity predominated in the east and south (probably, in most areas, associated also with a pattern of younger and more universal marriage – though this is somewhat speculative at present) while in northern Europe a more locally diverse pattern was found. Even within the complex areas different patterns have been discovered. In Russian-dominated serf areas of the East, figures of over 60 per cent of households with more than one conjugal core have been found, but in some parts of Hungary and north Italy the figure reached only 40 per cent while in central France it seldom exceeded 30 per cent [1]. Suggestions have also been made that while the south of France was characterised by a more truly stem-family system, in the central areas a system based on co-residence of married brothers was more important.

The picture of household composition, therefore, grows increasingly complex as more work is done on hitherto unstudied areas. It begins to look as if very different principles governed family formation in different areas of the pre-industrial West, but just what these were and why they varied as they did is so far little understood.

(c) *Le Mal des Moyennes (Flandrin in* [7]*) – or the Meaningless Mean*

Most of the figures on household composition, and particularly those worked by the Cambridge Group, have been produced at a community level of analysis (for example mean household sizes for each community, or proportions of households in each community which were of various structural types – conjugal, extended and so on). The reasons for proceeding in this way have on several occasions been stressed by Laslett when he has emphasised the lack of detail in most English listings on such topics as age, occupation and even relationships to household head. Nevertheless, both the particular indicators used and the emphasis on community-level statistics have been attacked.

Superficially, mean household sizes of fewer than 6 persons and situations where more than 80 per cent of households contained no non-conjugal kin seem clear evidence of the absence of a stem-family system in pre-industrial European populations. In fact this is not necessarily the case. Firstly, community-level statistics give a misleading impression by concealing one of the essential features of family life, the changing composition of the household over the life cycle. This criticism has been particularly associated with the work of Lutz Berkner who, analysing peasant families in one area of eighteenth-century Austria, was able to demonstrate that, while only 25 per cent of all households contained any kin, 60 per cent of households headed by men aged 18–27 did so, compared

30

with only 9 per cent of households headed by men aged 48–57 [68; see also his valuable discussion in 36]. Berkner, by the use of a range of supporting documentary material, was able to relate this pattern to one of the fundamental features of a stem-family system, the process of transfer of land between generations. If we imagine a household where land is transferred to a son on his marriage and the son subsequently has children of his own, then, if this occurs before his father's death, a three-generation family will appear in a census listing. A few years later, when the father has died, only a widow, married child and grand-children will be left and the evidence for a stem household becomes ambiguous. On the widow's death, a nuclear household will result and the census listing will reveal no evidence of any extension at all. Nevertheless – and this is the crucial point – while no stem-family *household* is pre-sent, a stem-family *organisation* remains since, in due course, the same process will be repeated by the next generation. Indeed, even where no stem-family system is in operation the availability of data on ages frequently shows a marked life-cycle effect in household data which is not apparent in aggregate data.

Now of course the extent to which a life-cycle pattern of residence like that described by Berkner will be concealed in figures showing mean household size or proportion of households in a community with co-resident kin will, to a great extent, depend on levels of fertility and mortality being experienced in the area and on the ages at which marriage occurs. In fact, subsequent research has sug-gested that mean household size is as sensitive to varying fertility and mortality levels as to rules of household formation and is thus almost useless as an indicator of family processes. Certainly very large mean household sizes are never to be expected in pre-industrial European populations. Equally a number of calculations have been made which suggest that the age at losing parents was so young in the past (in some areas three-quarters of males had no father alive at the time of their marriage) that the maximum proportion of households containing two lin-eally related ever-married adults likely to arise in stable historic Western populations was below 30 per cent (the

31

maximum possible anywhere is about 50 per cent). Thus, by
no means everyone could ever have appeared on census-
type listings as a member of a three-generation household
(though the maximum proportions would have been subject to considerable variations dependent on the demographic situation, a point usually ignored in comparative
analysis – though note [1: ch. 5]).

It is against this kind of background that Berkner has felt
able to conclude that a stem-family system was in operation
in an Austrian community where 25 per cent of all
households were in some sense extended [68] as well as in
an area of seventeenth-century Germany where 28 per cent
of households fitted his criteria [67]; he has also suggested
that such a phase could have occurred in England but has
been concealed in aggregate analysis [35]. However, recent
more sophisticated work by Wachter, Hammel and Laslett
[20] has employed advanced computer-simulation techniques, using historical demographic parameters to produce
estimates of the overall frequencies of different household
forms which would have occurred under various precisely
specified sets of rules governing the establishment of
complex households. This work has cast serious doubt on
the conclusions to be drawn even from some of Berkner's
own data (and indeed, even on the reliability of the sources
used) while demonstrating categorically that a multigener-
ational phase can never have been a significant phenomenon in pre-industrial England (indeed the fact that all the
variation in structure between studied English communities can be explained away in terms of random demographic events strongly supports the view that England
had a homogeneous nuclear-oriented system). Developments of this simulation technique will have important
impact on this area of family history in the future.

However, there is a third line of attack which will be less
easy to meet by community-level simulations. A number of
scholars have raised important questions about the validity
of analyses of household composition which ignore possible
variations between socio-economic groups and produce
what they argue are largely meaningless means [7; 35]. After
all, they say, the stem family is meant to be a feature of
peasant life and even in peasant societies by no means

everyone has ever been a peasant. Laslett himself had indeed shown in his original analysis of pre-1821 communities that the mean size of gentry households was 6.63 compared with 5.91 for yeoman farmers and 4.51 for labourers; for the same groups the respective percentages of households with kin were 28, 17 and 8. Other work has shown a strong correlation between complex households and size of agricultural holdings in a range of places from nineteenth-century Lancashire and Norway to Austria and elsewhere. This evidence strongly suggests that different groups of the population were either operating with different rules regarding household formation or, perhaps more likely, that some were more able than others to achieve particular objectives. If either of these were the case, then aggregate data at community level cannot be used to throw much meaningful light on the processes operating to produce patterns of household composition in the past (compare Hareven in [17] for a similar argument relating to other aspects of family composition). In the first case there was not one set of household-formation rules operating in the community but several (and even computer simulation cannot help to elucidate them if it operates at a community level of analysis). In the second case, a rule or ideal might be present as a governing principle of household formation even if it was seldom attained except, perhaps, by an opinion-forming élite. Stem-family ideals (or indeed any other set of rules encouraging the establishment of complex households) could then have been the organising principle underlying behaviour; such behaviour could be understood only by reference to them even if, in practice, only a minority of households at any time would have attained their objectives. These arguments have a certain intellectual attraction – and in so far as they relate to occupational differences they can be extended also to work derived from parish registers.

(d) *The Problem of Meaning*

We turn now to an altogether different and more fundamental set of limitations of a demographic approach and to a set of problems which extend beyond household analysis

33

(where they have been most explored) to any area of family – and indeed of social – history as soon as we try to use quantifiable observations to help us understand social behaviour. Problems of meaning arise at two levels. The first, the problem of the meaning of the behaviour to the person who recorded it, has already been referred to in the context of our ignorance of the purposes for which listings were prepared. Thus, the conclusions to be drawn from discovering that one town has many households with lodgers while another has not must depend on how those who drew up the lists defined 'lodger' and on how they distinguished one household from another. If this point is missed, however precise the rules that we draw up to ensure comparability in analysis of different listings, the comparisons are entirely spurious. A similar problem would arise with illegitimacy if there were changes or differences between areas in what was treated as a marriage and, therefore, in what was considered an illegitimate birth [47; 48; compare 1:*130–2* on English data]. This actually happened over the eighteenth and nineteenth centuries in Sweden.

However, the problem of what was meant by the recorder is only one part of a wider problem of what the behaviour meant to contemporaries in general. There is a constant and natural temptation to make inferences from demographic behaviour to attitudes which may – or may not – have underlain it. Some examples of this are Laslett's assertions that a narrow age-gap between spouses has meant that marriage has tended 'towards the companionate' [1:*13*] and his implicit assumption that we can conclude that illegitimacy rates are an indication of 'how often breaches of the familial regulations actually took place' [1:*103*], even though we know nothing about how those involved actually perceived familial morality. Such inferences based on no evidence on attitudes are at best dangerous and at worst highly misleading.

However, it is in the context of household composition that critics have drawn most attention to this problem. For Laslett, the long-run 'perdurance' and widespread distribution of a nuclear-household system is one of the key characteristics of the Western familial system. A number of other scholars, by contrast, have suggested that the variability of attitudes which could have (and arguably actually have) occurred within a nuclear-household framework is of infinitely greater significance than the stability of the framework itself. To ignore the fact that in one era in some social groups a co-residing grandmother may have been a revered and powerful matriarch, in another was housed only with extreme reluctance with everyone hoping that she would soon die, while in another she is viewed as an old friend who can claim the rights of friendship but no more, is, to these scholars, to miss the most essential changes which have occurred in familial systems over the past 500 years [compare 4; Anderson in 16]. Indeed, these scholars would probably argue that these differences and changes, in as far as they occurred, have been at least as significant as the differences between familial relationships in two areas (say north and south France) where the structure of the peasant household appears very different.

Not only, however, in the opinion of these critics, is an understanding of how individuals or community or state institutions saw familial behaviour important if we are to be able to undertake a meaningful comparative analysis, it is also necessary if we are to arrive at a valid interpretation of particular historical situations. While simulation exercises will show us if particular rules were *not* being successfully followed they can never show us what rules *were* followed nor, except tangentially, whether individuals were orienting their behaviour to, but not succeeding in keeping to, a particular set of rules. Simple statistics on household composition (or on anything else) can never tell us the meaning and expectations associated with behavioural acts. Indeed, in throwing doubt on the existence of a stem-familial rule Laslett himself lays great stress on the absence of any terminological or other cultural evidence of extended forms – though without citing the research base for his argument.

Even more problematical, of course, is the crucial question of whether rules governing a particular *household* form (as opposed for example to rules governing inheritance or treatment of distressed kin or methods of cropping land) has always or even usually been part of the Western tradition; certainly for scholars using the household economics approach (see chapter 4), household composition is seen largely as a by-product of other more fundamental processes. It must even be questioned whether the stem family as defined by LePlay is primarily or even significantly about residence at all. There are clear dangers in making inferences (as Laslett has done [34]) from household forms to familial forms [compare 35] and the fact that the household data are rigorously obtained should not lead us to exaggerate their importance or what we are entitled to infer from them.

(e) *The Problem of Theory*

This point, however, brings us to the final set of criticisms that have been raised of work within this tradition. The problems raised here are not so much those of what household composition or illegitimacy or marriage or child-bearing meant to participants as to whether the significance of data on them to the comparative historian should be treated as constant and non-problematical over time and between cultures.

Firstly, and most simply, there is the problem of whether a knowledge of household composition always tells us the same set of things – or even anything very much – about familial behaviour. Much familial behaviour in most societies takes place with non-co-resident kin while other behaviour involves only some members of a co-resident unit rather than the members of the unit as a whole. For many family activities, therefore, the precise composition of the domestic group will be irrelevant. Moreover, if certain crucial functions of the family change over time – as most scholars would agree that they have – then the significance of the domestic group for familial functions and for the family's relations with the outside world is likely to change also. So to compare household composition under two different sets of conditions without regard for these wider changes is to engage in a sterile exercise devoid of social meaning. Indeed, to focus too much attention on demographically based comparisons is to miss many of the most important changes in the ways in which family and kinship function in particular societies [58; 35; Anderson in

16]. Similar arguments about differences in the way in which behaviour fits into the wider social context (and is likely therefore to be of very different theoretical significance in different societies) could equally be made about much of the demographically oriented work on such topics as the age of marriage or illegitimacy.

This leads us to a final point. In general demographically oriented work has treated family behaviour in isolation from its socioeconomic setting, and in its comparative analysis of structure has ignored the clearly variable implications for both individual and society of the same family forms and rates of behaviour in different economic and political settings [35; 73; 37; Anderson in 16]. This tendency to treat the family in isolation from the wider social structure and to ignore the very different ways in which the same pattern of household structure or marriage rates or ages come about has been seen as a central limitation of the whole work of the school and is best explored in detail in chapter 4 where the focus is specifically on the work of those who have seen marriage and household structure as indicators or as results or even by-products of processes of production and reproduction.

By contrast, the demographic approach typically sees these rates and structures as 'social facts' meaningful in themselves. Not only does the treatment of household and family behaviour in isolation from the wider social structure (memorably described on one occasion as 'demography in a thermos flask') produce a very superficial kind of comparability based only on outward form, it also has had important implications for the methods adopted. Communities for study have been selected on the basis of the quality of their demographic evidence rather than for their theoretical contribution to problems and the availability of data on other aspects of the social structure; comparative categories have almost never been derived on the basis of any theory about how family behaviour might have related to other aspects of social life (such as inheritance practices, productive systems, land tenure or even population density). (Thus, for example, consider Laslett's analysis of illegitimacy in England where he says he 'has divided the 100 sets of passable recordings *quite arbitrarily* into five areas of the country' [1:*133* – my emphasis].) Moreover, where non-familial variables have been used, either rather simple models relating population to resources have typically been employed or largely unsuccessful attempts have been made to correlate community-level social and economic characteristics with community-level familial behaviour indicators; little effort has gone into exploring the possible impact of socioeconomic change via its impact on the internal relations of the families involved (compare Levine's general criticism [74] of much recent work in historical demography).

We are at this point on the fringes of a major debate over the methodology of history and over the possibility and limitations of theoretically oriented history. Perhaps somewhat ironically, for all their conscious imitation of social scientific method, the demographic group finds itself much closer to a traditional historical method than to the social sciences proper; for most modern social scientists would reject any 'empiricist' notion of facts independent of the theoretical and meaning-bound framework within which they were being considered. Recent sociological work, in particular, has emphasised the crucial importance of meaning and of the need to attempt to build a theoretically based understanding of the underlying processes which have generated the behaviour which is observed.

Yet it is easy to criticise the Cambridge Group and other leading writers within the demographic tradition without remembering the unsystematic and impressionistic studies that preceded their work and without also considering the serious problems which have been met by alternative approaches. Moreover, the techniques, many of the questions and, above all, the body of data which has been assembled lay at very least some outer bounds to the more speculative conclusions of scholars working in other traditions. There can be no doubt that the work of this school will have a lasting influence on the development of family history.

3 The Sentiments Approach

THE authors of the work to be discussed in this chapter all to a greater or lesser extent reject the argument that the crucial changes in the Western family over the past 500 years can be deduced from a limited range of demographic sources. Indeed the dominant figures seem to take the extreme view that a proper understanding of family history requires us to be mainly concerned not with stability or change in structure but with changes in meanings, not with 'the family as a reality but the family as an idea' [8:7] or as Shorter puts it: 'Many constellations of sentiment . . . are possible within any given structure, and because the crisis of the family today is a crisis of emotion – of attachment and rejection – it is incumbent upon the family historian to trace the tale of sentiments' [2:19].

The literature in this area is dominated by four general surveys of at least a major part of our period: Ariès's *Centuries of Childhood* [8], Shorter's *Making of the Modern Family* [2], Stone's *Family, Sex and Marriage in England 1500–1800* [4] and (though his work has wider relevance) Flandrin's *Families in Former Times* [7]. (Note also the many parallel approaches in [9 and 10].) Though I shall introduce other material, much of this chapter is concerned with a review of these four works. At a superficial level there are many differences between their analyses; yet their methodologies, interpretations and broad conclusions have much in common and they also share many weaknesses.

The common interests can most clearly be seen in their basic concern with the emergence of 'modern' social relationships. However, this concern with the present raises a particularly intractable set of problems. In recent years sociologists have increasingly seen the modern family as a web of symbols and ideas, partly created by the participants

39

themselves and partly by certain professional interest groups aided by the mass media. They have thus pointed to the constraining effects of the assumptions which we today make about sex, childhood, parenthood and kinship and to the symbolic significance of ideas like 'home', 'privacy' and even 'family' itself. Inevitably, therefore, a concern with the origins of these ideas and assumptions has become a central problem for this approach; but this leads to serious problems of evidence.

The demographic approach started from a particular set of documents, by which their questions and conclusions have been constrained. These sentiments writers began with a set of questions about the ideas associated with family behaviour and were then faced with the problem of finding suitable source material to throw light on such ideas. Even those like Stone, Flandrin and Ariès who have been most concerned with material relating to and produced by the literate minority – diaries, contemporary accounts, religious and imaginative literature, and artifacts such as domestic architecture, toys and paintings – have faced difficulties in identifying and discriminating the timings of shifts in attitudes. This problem is made worse by regional and socioeconomic differences in sentiments at any one point in time, by the fact that in any group of the population more than one set of attitudes can be current at the same period (nicely demonstrated for child-rearing in eighteenth-century North America by [57]), and by the fact that attitudes do not change overnight, so that old and new forms can continue side by side for a century or more. Thus, the identification of significant trends is difficult even for scholars of the literate minority. Since, in addition, more than one interpretation can often be put on any one scrap of evidence and all literary statements need to be interpreted carefully in the light of the social and cultural context to which they relate, the judgement of the individual scholar is particularly important (the best clear statement of these problems can be found in [9]). Moreover it is particularly difficult to demonstrate categorically the emergence of *new* patterns of behaviour because of the need to decide whether the behaviour really was new at a particular period or, alternatively, had simply begun for the first time at that period to appear in the available sources.

As soon as attention is turned to the sentiments of ordinary people the source problems have proved almost insuperable because of uncertainty about the reliability of the assertions of local doctors, minor bureaucrats, ethnographers and folklorists of the time, who provide the main sources which have been so far used. Any attempt to build a coherent picture from this assemblage of random information is bound to be tentative and to involve leaps of imagination at times; too often, however, the problem has been made worse by a style of writing in which speculation or even pure fantasy is glossed over as if it were clearly established fact; a huge edifice covering, in Shorter's case, half a continent, is sometimes built on a few scraps of information (which in both Stone's and Shorter's work is sometimes culled from a different century or included with scant regard for possible regional or social-class differences in behaviour – indeed, Stone's whole discussion of the English masses is so feebly based that it can safely be ignored).

These are serious criticisms. Nevertheless these scholars almost alone have published work on these issues of meaning and, on many themes, the body of evidence that they have assembled is strong enough at least to pose a challenge to others to find new sources and develop new ways of undertaking this essential task. For example, all point to the growing discreteness of the conjugal family (parents and their unmarried children) as a social group. Particularly interesting in this connection is evidence on changing definitions of the word 'family' in contemporary dictionaries which only in the late eighteenth and early nineteenth centuries lay major stress on the conjugal couple and their children, as opposed to definitions stressing either the whole household including servants or the whole kinship group. Reviewing the evidence, Flandrin concludes that 'the concept of the family, . . . as it is most commonly defined today, has only existed in our western culture since a comparatively recent date.' [7:9; see also 10] A similar point has been taken even further by Hanssen [87] who has argued that among Scandinavian peasants everyday behaviour was probably much more oriented to the productive or residential group and to working and neighbourhood relationships than to the conjugal family.

Regardless of whether this extreme position is valid outside Scandinavia, there is general agreement among writers of this school that in the sixteenth century the notion of the nuclear group as a clearly differentiated unit, with a recognised right to maintain its differentiation through norms of privacy, was absent among almost all sections of the population. Indeed, it is often argued [2; 4; 7] that, at least in propertied groups, not merely was the conjugal family not recognised as having an independent existence but, for most important purposes, the rights and expectations of the individual were subsumed within those of a wider kindred (though as far as formal legal rights are relevant – which some scholars would in part question – this position is properly challenged for England by Macfarlane [89]).

Perhaps most important of all, however, is the stress laid on the embedded position of the individual and household in the wider community [4], on the abundance of strong non-familial relationships (which if nothing else made the family *relatively* less important [7; 8]), and on a sense of communality whereby 'members of the family felt that they had more in common emotionally with their various peer groups than with one another' [2:5]. Moreover, it is widely stressed that not only was the family not a clearly discrete group but its members had no significant right to privacy. Within the household a general 'promiscuity' [7] prevailed. The continual presence of outsiders both residential (servants) and others (for example, business partners and clients), together with a form of domestic architecture which made little provision (except minimally in bed) for privacy even among the rich (the poor had little opportunity within their tiny houses for privacy anyway), are all seen as militating against any possibility of the development of modern familial sentiments.

The extent of community-based interference and supervision (made easier by the minute size of most settlements and the need in many areas for co-operation in agricultural activities [Braun in 18; 87]) is similarly stressed, Stone arguing that it increased in England in the seventeenth century; factors mentioned include the public rituals to which newly married couples were subjected [8], the role of local secular authorities (involving in England the right of a local constable to break into any house where he suspected fornication or adultery to be occurring [4] and in parts of central Europe powers to control all aspects of leisure activity [2]), the powers of local religious courts fed by a continual supply of gossip [4; 66; 2], and various forms of institutionalised popular ridicule expressed through rough music or 'charivari' designed to bring into line those who had breached popularly held views of family morality [Thompson in *Annales E.S.C.* 1972].

Central to the arguments of this group of authors is a picture of family relationships markedly different from those of later periods. Thus in the sixteenth century – and much later in many areas – family behaviour is seen as characterised by strong elements of deference, patriarchy and authoritarianism. The power of husband over wife and children is widely cited, being concerned not only with economic matters but also with moral control including the right – indeed in some areas apparently the duty [7] – to use physical force on wife and children. The inferior legal position of women was paralleled by limitations in many areas on children's ability to enter into contracts until well into their twenties (if then) while their right either in law or in practice to select their own spouses was often strictly circumscribed.

Another widely stressed theme is a markedly low level of affection, Stone's impression, indeed, being of a society where almost everyone found it difficult to establish any emotional ties, where violence came easily and no one was to be trusted (a picture, however, denied by Macfarlane [5]). Flandrin, basing his analysis on a study of confessors' manuals, finds no evidence of a duty to love (in the modern sense) either spouse or children; instead there is a marked emphasis on respect, on deference and obligation, while affection and sentimental attachments are treated with suspicion and seen as likely to lead to disorder.

The effect of these attitudes on familial relationships is, then, clear. Among the upper classes Stone portrays marriage as remote, with spouses having separate sets of rooms, staff and daily lives, being only rarely together in private. Among peasants Shorter sees marital relationships as characterised by distance and formality – in France he notes that couples stopped using 'tu' on their wedding day and adopted the formal form of address 'vous' – with the subordination of women symbolised by their standing while their husbands ate. Marriage was, he suggests, seen as an economic, productive and reproductive rather than an emotional relationship, a mechanism for transmitting property and position from generation to generation. Sex in marriage is portrayed as a sinful necessity justified only by the need to propagate the species [4; 2] and as a duty which the wife could not refuse even if she would suffer as a result [7]. Both Shorter and Flandrin infer from rapid remarriage that little emotional commitment was involved in marriage and this argument is strengthened by a consideration of the criteria used in spouse selection.

Taking this general picture as a starting point the major authors in this school describe a gradual movement away from this relatively emotionless, open, undifferentiated and patriarchal family. An increasing individualism was associated with increasing differentiation of the conjugal family as a discrete and private social unit and with a growing emphasis on individual autonomy and rights. At the same time the role of familial interest declined and an increasing emphasis was placed on emotion as the prime basis of family relationships. For Stone the crucial change is that 'from distance, deference and patriarchy to what I have chosen to call Affective Individualism' [4:4]. For Shorter and for Flandrin sentiment and consideration become increasingly important, for Ariès the physical and emotional well-being of the child becomes a central concern. Only Macfarlane [5; also 89] has seriously challenged this position, and then only its widespread applicability to England and perhaps North America. Macfarlane argues that parts of Stone's evidence are totally irrelevant to his case and that Stone could only have reached the conclusions that he did because he had certain preconceptions about the trends that he would find. Certainly Macfarlane's criticisms together with the small amounts of evidence that

44

he has produced do suggest that Stone has oversimplified the changes he describes. On the other hand, it would be premature to argue – as Macfarlane seems to imply – that nothing much really changed at all, at least among the aristocracy, squirearchy and parts of the higher middle classes; certainly there is considerable evidence to suggest that certain forms of behaviour became more frequent while others were tending to die out (see [9] for a useful discussion here).

On the main trends our principal authors broadly agree. Where they do not always agree is on chronology, on the groups in society where changes came first and, above all, on the causes of the changes. Also, while Shorter and Ariès portray a linear trend – in Shorter's terms from 'traditional' to 'modern' – Flandrin portrays a regionally complex pattern even within the confines of France, while Stone's account contains a period of 'regression' for some groups in the late sixteenth and in the seventeenth centuries and (though this is beyond the end of his detailed period of research) a major reversal in the nineteenth century to a pattern much more like that of several centuries earlier.

The detail of their arguments is best assessed in a series of separate sections.

(i) THE SEGREGATION OF THE CONJUGAL UNIT – PRIVACY AND DOMESTICITY

Shorter writes: 'The nuclear family is a state of mind rather than a particular kind of structure or set of household arrangements. . . . What really distinguishes the nuclear family . . . from other patterns of life in Western society is a special sense of solidarity that separates the domestic unit from the surrounding community' [2:205]. On the same theme Ariès writes that the 'seventeenth century family was not the modern family: it was distinguished from the latter by the enormous mass of sociability which it retained' [8:390]. Over the past four centuries this permeability of the family changed, first probably among the bourgeiosie and the squirearchy and most recently among the labouring masses and the aristocracy, first probably in North America and England in the seventeenth century, later in

France at the end of the eighteenth century and still later in parts of Eastern Europe.

In part, it is argued, this happened because external social controls decreased beginning in the sixteenth century in some places but accelerating through the later seventeenth and eighteenth centuries. Religious motivations to control family behaviour lessened as Puritan doctrines with their almost overwhelming concern with family morality declined. The power of the local ecclesiastical and manorial courts was eroded in the same period though in some parts of central Europe community authorities obtained stronger powers (notably to prevent marriages among the labouring poor who might become potential paupers) until some time in the nineteenth century; the Law of Settlement was similarly used at times in England. Similarly it was the nineteenth century or even later before one of the main informal institutions of community control – the charivari – completely disappeared from many areas. Finally, though not for England or probably North America where population turnover had always been high, attention has been drawn to the potential impact of increased in- and out-migration and growing size of settlement; equally importantly, people came from, and went to, settlements further away, thus making their behaviour much more difficult to supervise.

In parallel with these external changes there went an increasing appreciation of privacy (on this general topic see [52]). In part this can be seen in a fall in street and community life with reduced involvement in festivals and other community-based activities, though this was, of course, particularly important in the lower classes. Inside the home, too, changes occurred. Domestic architecture changed with a segregation between rooms for sleeping, eating, and conducting business, while the introduction of corridors was particularly important in creating space where more affluent families could be secure from the intrusion of strangers and, later, of servants [see also 53]; the fall in the numbers of living-in farm servants and the increasing segregation of domestic servants from the meals and sleeping apartments of their masters' families were a topic of much comment in eighteenth-century England and

46

were seen by contemporaries as associated with new aspir-
ations (particularly by wives) for a more private and status-
differentiated existence [see also 87 on Sweden]. Flandrin,
for France in the sixteenth to the eighteenth centuries, also
stresses a rising, religiously inspired, emphasis on prudery
and a growing concern about the possible sexual consequences (for both daughters and sons in the household) of
promiscuous living arrangements (see [9] for an analogous
discussion relating to the English aristocracy in the eighteenth century). Interestingly, Modell and Hareven [39] see
similar pressures as important in the late nineteenth and
early twentieth centuries in the decline of lodging as a
normal feature of urban life, particularly in the United
States; with the eclipse of lodging the isolation of the
conjugal family was complete.

However, there is also a third element, a rising emphasis
on domesticity. Not merely was the conjugal family isolated,
it became an object of veneration as did the culture of 'true
domestic womanhood' which was largely associated with it.
French observers of the eighteenth century frequently
commented on the extent to which English gentlemen and
their wives were always together – except, of course, after
dinner – and pointed to the very different pattern in
France. By the nineteenth century domesticity in England
and North America had reached its zenith and spread to
other social groups. In the bourgeoisie it became associated
with a new set of sex-role ideologies involving the strict
segregation of work (performed by men away from home)
from domestic concerns (ideally performed in the home by
servants under the supervision of women). The home came
to be seen as a haven, a retreat from the pressures of a
capitalistically oriented competitive world (see also [88]). In
the United States, Sennett [77] has traced this development
down into the lower middle class and has argued that this
emphasis on the home as a retreat from the world of work
inhibited the proper socialisation of the young, as many
families cut themselves off almost entirely from the
involvement of any but a single male breadwinner in
experiences outside the domestic scene. In the working
classes too, by the late nineteenth century there was
emerging a cult of 'home sweet home', though here this

47

movement seems mainly based in a desire to preserve a little self-respect and secrecy ('keeping yourself to yourself') in what typically remained a public world of small, over-crowded houses, thin walls, public street life and precarious hold over respectability.

(ii) CHANGING ATTITUDES TO INTERPERSONAL RELATIONSHIPS

At the same time as they see an emphasis on increasing *family* autonomy and cohesiveness, however, these authors also see a growth in *individual* autonomy and rights. Flandrin calls it 'individualism within the bosom of the family' [7 : *110*] while Shorter describes a new set of values 'sanctioning individualism over community allegiance and self-realisation over collective solidarity' [2 : *21*]; for Shorter, at least, it was this new set of values ('a wish to be free') which were the prime movers in familial as well as wider social change.

Now clearly there is a long intellectual pedigree to the argument that an emerging individualism was an import-ant part of the great transformation of Western societies since the Middle Ages; the argument that this occurred first in England and North America is also not new (Macfarlane [89], by contrast, argues that any change in England had occurred long before the sixteenth century and was there-fore quite irrelevant as a source of possible familial change). What this group of family historians has done is to point to the implications of a rising individualism for relationships between members of the conjugal family, though the precise nature of this individualism is often obscure and the uses of the term seems to vary between different authors; even more unclear are the timing and precise social location of many of the changes (though see chapter 4). Neverthe-less some apparently clear evidence of a greater attention to individual rights appears among the bourgeoisie from the late seventeenth century in England and from the late eighteenth century in France. Clark points to the develop-ment among the rich of separate bedrooms for each child as a nineteenth-century culmination of a view of the family as a unit 'made up of separate units who each had a separate role to play . . . a vehicle for providing the development of each of its members' [53:52]. Elsewhere both Stone and Flandrin stress changes in property arrangements which increased the autonomy of the child, a change reinforced in England from the late seventeenth century by a decline in the religious emphasis on the father as spiritual head of the family. Both authors also stress increasing freedom of wives and children from physical punishment and point to an increasingly reciprocal basis of parent-child relationships and marriage, with a recognition of women's rights to consideration. Stone also claims to identify a changing attitude to death; as people became more than their roles the death of a near relative became a personal loss.

This greater emotionalism in attitudes to death is it-self one manifestation of the second important change in interpersonal relations, a shift in balance away from interest and towards sentiment [4; 2; 7]. Stone and Shorter, in particular, emphasise the increasing stress on the pursuit of happiness as a goal, marriage becoming for more people a source of pleasure, both emotional and sexual. Children, too, are seen (by all four of our principal scholars) as ben-efiting from a warmer, more sensitive familial environ-ment. It is easiest to explore the detailed implications of these arguments in separate discussions of spouse selection, marriage, sex, and children.

(iii) SPOUSE SELECTION

The argument for major transformations both in how spouse selection has taken place and in the criteria used for selection has been particularly pursued by Stone, Trum-bach and Shorter (though there are important differences between their arguments).

Briefly, Shorter suggests that, starting in the late eight-eenth century among the working classes, a 'romantic revolution' began in which personal choice and expressive considerations replaced instrumental criteria as the main basis of spouse selection. This pattern spread across classes and societies in the nineteenth century to become dominant in the twentieth; an essential by-product of this revolution was the collapse of traditional institutions of control by family and community over courtship. However, his analysis leaves many loose ends. For example, he makes no serious attempt to resolve the ambiguity over the relative roles of parents and peers; on the one hand, he describes courtship institutions almost totally controlled by peer groups; yet he also continually emphasises the power of parents, and it is often unclear just how the two mesh together. He may be using evidence from different regions or different social groups where practices really were different; alternatively there may have been real ambiguity in actual experience. Unfortunately, here as elsewhere Shorter's plausible enough case is supported by a haphazard collection of data from different areas and periods and no contextually clear picture emerges.

The picture presented by Stone is altogether more complex. He distinguishes three elements in control over spouse selection: whether parents or child take the initiative, how much veto the other party has and, though he perhaps understresses its importance, the institutions regulating meeting and courtship. On criteria for selection he distinguishes four discrete elements: 'interest', 'mutual affection' (associated with well-tried and solidly based friendship and companionship), 'romance', and 'sexual attraction'; he argues that each of these in turn increased in relative importance while none was ever totally replaced. Stone, however, (and here he differs significantly from Shorter) also differentiates between a popular awareness of romantic love and sexual attraction as *motives for pair bonding* and their use as *mate selection criteria*. He points out that romantic and sexual love were part of popular literature at least by the sixteenth century but argues (though on the basis of minimal evidence) that, certainly for the higher social groups, they were treated largely as fantasy; and he is correctly concerned to stress also the continuing importance of material considerations – for example, economic prospects or domestic abilities – as significant factors in mate choice today. Stone thus suggests not so much a replacement of one set of values by another as a shift in the relative emphasis laid on a more or less constant set – and also to some extent only a relative shift in the power balance between parents and children. Equally plausibly (though his

50

evidence is very thin) Stone suggests that there have always been major differences between socioeconomic groups; he is probably right, but his fourteen-line discussion of the possibility that parents among the 'labouring poor' had no power as early as the sixteenth century does even less justice to the problem than his brief but better documented argument that the English squirearchy retained considerable power until well into the nineteenth.

The issues involved in this debate are complex, though good-quality evidence is minimal. The most plausible evidence would, however, indicate a picture something like the following. Whenever and wherever parents have controlled resources vital to their children's future standard of living they have been able to influence strongly their children's choice of spouses. This was the case for most middle- and upper-class groups until the late nineteenth century and remains so in many peasant areas even today. By contrast, among the wage-earning classes this power has always been much less important. Parental power was also less important in the past in those peasant areas where parents had little discretion over which of their children were to inherit [7; Braun in 18].

Parents also differed in the extent of motivations to intervene in their children's courtships. Such motivations have been strong in peasant societies where incoming daughters had to live with or near (and often had to help support) their parents-in-law in old age, and also where dowries provided marriage opportunities for siblings. Intervention was also encouraged by situations where political or financial or commercial alliances could be sealed by marriage; particularly in the eighteenth and nineteenth centuries before Limited Liability made it redundant, the marriage alliance was often used by the commercial classes to keep property in the family (via first-cousin marriage) or to provide finance for business enterprise [49; 50]. Finally, a variety of courtship institutions have operated to assist parents (or peers) in controlling who met whom, and who was put in a position where courtship could legitimately commence; bundling and village dances were important for peasants and rural labourers in many parts of continental Europe until the mid-nineteenth century or even later.

51

Other sources stress the importance of go-betweens; indeed they are probably still important in certain areas. For the middle and upper classes more formal rituals and procedures such as chaperonage, press advertising of available dowries and, for the élite, events like the London Season [51] became more important in the late eighteenth and early nineteenth centuries and remained so for a century at least.

As far as criteria of spouse choice are concerned the picture is equally complex. Even if we accept that instrumental factors – or interest – were more important in the earlier part of our period, it seems useful to distinguish between externally oriented interests (those of parents, relatives and the wider community in guaranteeing suitable maintenance in old age, or in bringing honour or perquisites or business to the family) and interests immediately relevant to those involved (for example, the selection of a spouse who was able to make a direct economic contribution by working with her husband, by bringing substantial savings into the marriage, or even by not being so fertile that the producer-consumer balance was upset). The first category of interest was undoubtedly significant in upper-bourgeois and aristocratic circles in the sixteenth and seventeenth centuries [4; 9] and may in some places have increased in the eighteenth and nineteenth among commercial groups [7]. However, particularly among the solid middle classes, a second idea began from an early date to gain strength, one which emphasised the importance of 'joining of hearts' and 'knitting together of affections'; by the eighteenth century La Rochefoucauld (cited by several authorities) can be observed noting that three-quarters of English middle- and upper-class marriages were based on companionship and friendship, though at this period this kind of marriage was still very much a minority in France. But, of course, such emotions were still strictly channelled along economic lines, being permitted to develop only within a restricted field of eligibles [compare 7].

In peasant families by contrast, at least in areas where parents passed on a plot to one or more children *pre-mortem* in return for support and also had power to control spouse selection, the emergence of a greater emphasis on friendship, companionship and romance in spouse selection seems hardly to have been relevant at all [compare 43]; the old instrumental criteria were still being stressed in rural Ireland in the 1930s [62] and apparently in parts of Germany in the post-war period.

(iv) THE FUNCTIONS OF MARRIAGE

That any change at all became a realistic possibility for the mass of the population reflects, in the opinion of writers of this school, a major alteration in the functions of marriage and, with it, in the nature of marital relationships. The prime functions of marriage today are of an intrinsic, affective kind, and historians of the sentiments school see the relative importance of intrinsic functions as dramatically rising over the past 500 years, partly as economic functions became less important [see also Smelser in 19] and partly as the provision of these functions outside the family has declined. Marriage before the seventeenth century is seen as formal and tied up with extrinsic functions, that is to say sheer survival for the masses, production and reproduction for the peasantry, and familial advancement for the higher social groups. However, change appeared from at least the seventeenth century in England and North America [4; 7; 66], and from the late eighteenth century in France [7]. Among the middle classes, companionship, life-long affection and, slightly later, an 'honourable' sexual dimension (husbands being expected to behave like lovers, as Flandrin puts it) entered marriage, and sex came to be seen not as a duty (with its enjoyment as a temptation to mortal sin), but in its modern role of expressing, sustaining and strengthening love. For these scholars the sexual prudery of some sections of the nineteenth-century middle classes was not a continuation of earlier 'traditional' behaviour but a reversion, brought about perhaps by the Evangelical revival [4] and perhaps by a reflection into domestic life of the materialistic and hierarchical relationships of a capitalist economy.

By contrast, for Shorter, this emergence of sentiment, romance and sexuality had its roots firmly in the working classes, as the young increasingly broke free from tra-

53

ditional constraints and followed their own emotional and sexual inclinations. Since, for Shorter, changing attitudes to sexuality are used as important evidence of a surge of romantic sentiment (so that he would, for example, miss the primarily non-sexually manifested shifts in attitudes of the Victorian middle classes) his arguments are best dealt with in the next section.

(v) ILLEGITIMACY AND CHANGING ATTITUDES TO SEX

As I noted in chapter 2, the history of illegitimacy and premarital sex in the West is a history of cycles. From a low point in the seventeenth century the rates generally rose to a high in the mid-nineteenth, fell in the Second World War and rose dramatically thereafter. The explanation of these changes is a topic of major controversy among family historians, though all reject the superficially plausible proposition that illegitimacy rose at times when pregnancy-provoked marriages fell, and vice versa, because premarital conceptions and the illegitimacy indicators in fact move together (except, sometimes, over short periods of time).

A number of recent interpretations suggest that major changes in attitudes to sexuality were involved in these shifts in non-marital sexual behaviour. However, because data on attitudes to sex are so hard to come by, the main burden of the case in their favour comes by default, by a rejection by their authors of alternative explanations. For example, improvements in the reliability of reporting or in popular or official ideas about what constituted a marriage could significantly have affected illegitimacy rates but, except possibly between the mid-sixteenth and mid-seventeenth centuries, such effects are unlikely to have been of major significance in most countries. Similarly, while rates of stable extramarital cohabitation have undoubtedly varied over time (being particularly high in some urban areas in the nineteenth century), only a small part of the overall change in most countries is likely to have resulted from them. Another possible set of explanations would be changes in people's biological ability to bear children (fecundity), or in the use of contraception or in

54

abortion, abandonment or infanticide. For the rise in illegitimacy between the seventeenth and the nineteenth centuries only fecundity changes seem relevant and it is very possible that a significant part of the first surge in illegitimacy could have been associated with fecundity change; the problem is that at present we do not really know how to test a proposition of this kind; certainly, it cannot have been the only factor at work.

The fall in illegitimacy and prenuptial pregnancy between the mid-nineteenth and mid-twentieth centuries, by contrast, has been attributed to the increased use of contraception in extramarital liasons [41], though the young and inexperienced are not usually very effective users of contraception. However, for Britain in particular this explanation of the nineteenth-century decline has to face a more serious objection. Fertility among married people first fell among the middle classes, in the last part of the nineteenth century [27], and little fall is observable in the rest of the population before the end of the century. A contraception-based explanation of the decline would require widespread use of contraception to have begun among the working-class unmarried who, however, made no substantial use of their discovery in marriage until half a century later. Until this objection can be overcome serious doubts remain as to the role of contraception in the nineteenth-century illegitimacy decline.

Another interesting proposition is one which suggests that changes have been due not to more sexual activity in any one section of the population but rather to changes in the proportion of the population who fell into the more sexually active groups. Stone, and Scott and Tilly [80; 42], for example, interpret the eighteenth- and nineteenth-century rise in this way, suggesting that the sectors of the population whose life chances were not controlled by property inheritance or the need to build up capital to set up a business had always been less inhibited sexually; since agricultural and industrial developments from the eighteenth century onwards led to a steady rise in the proportion of the population not inhibited in this way, the overall rise in illegitimacy could to a great extent be a statistical artifact. This is an important argument not usually considered in the past but once again there is little evidence one way or the other; what is needed is occupationally specific data on illegitimacy which preferably relates illegitimate conceptions to numbers at risk – and we have at present little data of this kind.

Even if there was a real increase in the propensity of women to have an illegitimate child, the question remains as to whether this resulted not from changes in attitudes but rather from changes in the social context in which courtship took place. If, for example, premarital sexual activity was a common feature of English pre-industrial courtship then fluctuations in illegitimacy could largely be due to the intervention of outside factors during courtship which temporarily or permanently frustrated an intention to get married by removing the ability of the couple to raise the cash necessary to establish a household of their own (or to finance appropriate wedding celebrations). Levine [74], in particular, has suggested that changes in the stability of grain prices and in Poor Law policy could largely explain the patterns he observes in his communities in the late eighteenth and early nineteenth centuries. This view of rising illegitimacy as a reflection of a rising incidence of frustrated marriage is also proposed by Scott and Tilly [42] for some areas of central Europe in the nineteenth century, though here it was local policy aimed at controlling poverty which was responsible.

Other explanations [Wrightson and Levine in 40; 74] point to changes in the nature and extent of control over the courtship behaviour of the masses by local élites and moral entrepreneurs. For example, Levine [74] suggests that the power and authority of Puritan élite groups grew in the later seventeenth century and that they set out to suppress traditional modes of behaviour including courtship; over the eighteenth century they became more tolerant of popular behaviour which was not actually politically threatening and greater freedom of action led to freer courtship and a higher risk of illegitimacy. Similar changes in external control have been observed in New England [45] in this period, while Phayer [43], for Bavaria, argues that the sudden rise c. 1800 was associated in great part with the abolition of community control following local government reorganisation and the removal of sanctions available to religious authorities.

A rather different view of changing external controls over courtship is proposed by Scott and Tilly [80; 42]. They argue that traditional courtship behaviour (involving as it normally did some element of premarital cohabitation) was carried over into transient urban situations which lacked the traditional familial, local community and church controls which had ensured in the past that marriages eventually ensued. Such a view has a great deal to commend it, particularly if similar breakdowns of community control can also be documented for rural areas [44; 46]; Phayer [43], however, rejects such an argument for his parts of rural France and Germany.

The arguments described so far do not attribute the fluctuations in illegitimacy to fundamental changes in attitudes to sexual behaviour. Scholars within the sentiments tradition, however, have nevertheless produced important arguments in favour of doing so. Several versions of this position can be identified. The first is proposed in slightly different forms by Flandrin, Phayer and Stone and emphasises the changing desire and ability of the Church to repress sexuality, by surrounding it with moral inhibitions. Flandrin, for example, notes the increasing attempts by the Church from the sixteenth century to suppress concubinage and to create a popular image of sex as a non-erotic duty rather than as something pleasurable. A similar argument, stressing the declining power of moral inhibitions over the masses during the eighteenth century, is put forward by Stone. These arguments are plausible but, yet again, there is the problem of establishing the historical connection between the relatively well-documented actions of religious authorities and almost totally inaccessible popular attitudes. Only Phayer's correlation of a sudden Bavarian rise in illegitimacy with the removal of religious sanctions is wholly convincing; the effect of this, Phayer argues, was to leave a moral vacuum in which sex could be freed from moral inhibitions even among the religious – or at least among those whose parents were unable to use economic means to control their courtship behaviour.

This problem of finding adequate evidence applies even

57

more strongly to Shorter's proposition that the major pre-twentieth-century surge in illegitimacy in Western societies resulted not simply from a fall in inhibitions but from something positive, from a transformation ('a sexual revolution') in popular attitudes to sex (in his earlier writings he called it a shift from 'manipulative' to 'expressive' sexuality [Shorter in 11]). For Shorter, then, the rise in illegitimacy requires, above all, an explanation of 'the willingness of young, unmarried women to abandon traditional chastity and instead go out with different men, have sex before marriage, and preoccupy themselves generally with personal happiness' [2:*260*]. And his answer lies in 'the new access to paid employment' which allowed rebellion against traditional restraints and not only permitted but also encouraged the seeking of pleasure and fulfillment in uninhibited sexual activity. Capitalist paid employment allowed private gratification to become more important than fitting into the common weal; 'the wish to be free produced the illegitimacy explosion' [2:*260*].

Not surprisingly, Shorter's arguments have come under attack. For example, it has been pointed out that Shorter's case, however superficially plausible, is largely based on posited connections between the historical events of increasing paid employment of women and rise in illegitimacy, without any attempt to document the intervening motivational processes involved. Other scholars have questioned whether there was any new large-scale 'access to paid employment' of a capitalist kind which involved the emancipation of women from traditional constraints [42]. Stone makes similar points when he suggests that those who had illegitimate children were much more likely to have been 'the poorest, the most ignorant, most defenceless and exploited of women, not cheerful hedonistic pleasure-seekers conjured up by modern sexual romantics' [4]. In other words, we need to know much more about *who* had the illegitimate babies, *where* and in *what contexts*, before we can start to argue that a new, capitalist-inspired, hedonistic individualism was responsible for the changes.

And yet it would be wrong to assume that attitudes to sex remained constant over the past 500 years. The question is how one should set out to identify and document what

58

changed where and when; and the problem of adequate
evidence may mean that on this important topic we shall
never really know – but that does not make the topic any
less important.

(vi) PARENTHOOD AND CHILDHOOD

'Good mothering is an invention of modernization. In
traditional society, mothers viewed the development and
happiness of infants younger than two with indifference. In
modern society, they place the welfare of their small
children above all else.' Thus, Edward Shorter opens his
discussion of changes in the attitudes and behaviour
associated with parenthood and childhood [2:*168*].

This issue was first raised as a central theme in Ariès's
Centuries of Childhood [8]. Briefly, the argument is as follows.
In medieval society the idea of childhood as a separate
phase in the human life cycle did not exist. Human beings,
once they could live without the constant solicitude of their
mothers, were part of adult society. They dressed like
adults, worked like adults, and even went to war with
adults – except that the concept 'adult' also hardly existed
in a society where social divisions were not age-graded but
status-graded and lay between married household heads
and their wives on the one hand, and all other persons old
enough to work on the other [compare 86]. Human beings
too fragile to participate in this 'adult' existence simply 'did
not count', indeed in an important sense were not seen as
'human' at all.

Ariès's subsequent discussion lacks precision over detail,
timing and, above all, social-class differences in the trends
he describes; it also fails to distinguish the two opposing
trends of detaching 'children' from 'adult' society and
turning 'infants' into 'children'. Nevertheless, his main
points are clear. On the one hand, there developed (for the
aristocracy and the educated from the seventeenth century)
specifically children's dress, toys, games, literature and new
attitudes to education so that childhood became increasingly separated from adulthood. On the other hand
attitudes to infants changed and they were seen more and
more as small human beings whose feelings could and

59

should be understood, who were to be played with like toys or pets, and above all to be enjoyed. Along with this went a second new theme, that children were a responsibility, fragile beings who needed to be understood and safeguarded, creatures with potential for good and evil who needed discipline to ensure that the innate evil was suppressed and the good fostered. The modern concept of parenthood, with its duties and obligations to child and society, was thus born (though many scholars would see a fully modern image of child development as emerging only in the late nineteenth century [Kaestle and Vinovskis in 19; 55; 88]). Trumbach and Stone [9; 4] confirm similar patterns before the eighteenth century for the bourgeoisie and upper classes in England, and similar trends have also been reported – again from an early date – in North America.

It is against this background that Ariès would have us interpret many of the child-rearing practices of earlier generations – the floggings, the swaddling, the leaving of infants for long periods alone, the widespread practices of putting children out to nurse, the lack of emotion at children's deaths (seen, probably quite rightly, by Macfarlane as open to some doubt at least as a universal phenomenon [5]), practices which continued among the working classes in many areas of Europe until the late eighteenth and even into the nineteenth century [8; 2]. But, given that behavioural changes occurred, how do we interpret them? Certainly it would be quite wrong to dismiss any possibility of attitudinal changes; ideas like parenthood and childhood are socially constructed and thus can be put together in as diverse a set of ways as those we use to construct our ideas about other mammals (think of the different popular images of the 'mentalities' of rats, cows and sheepdogs). The views of contemporary moralists changed over time, and new attitudes to children emerged in literature and drama. However, here, as with sexuality, major problems of interpretation arise from a lack of attitudinal data which relate to the mass of the population.

The problems raised by these issues can be seen particularly clearly in the criticisms which have been made of Shorter's attempts to explore changes in working-class attitudes to child-rearing. The quote which began this section, with its emphasis on the 'indifference' of traditional mothers, hints at a quite conscious set of mental processes. Compare also Shorter's description of sending children out to nurse: 'these mothers did not *care*, and that this is why their children vanished in the ghastly slaughter of the innocents that was traditional child-rearing' [2:*204*; emphasis in original].

But, as Sussman [56] has pointed out, there could be two alternative explanations of this behaviour. One is that out-nursing was believed to be safer in a period before reliable alternatives to breast feeding existed; the other is that it was inspired by overwhelming economic pressures. Sussman is able to demonstrate for France that the timing of changes is incompatible with Shorter's cultural model and with the 'safe alternatives' model, but that there was a heavy concentration of mothers of wet-nursed children in areas and trades which combined modest wages for men with, typically, household production involving an important role for women. Thus, for Sussman, the prime explanation of wet nursing lies in the necessity, if their families were not to starve, for married women to be involved in a form of work activity which by its nature largely inhibited breast feeding [compare 7]. Attitudes to children would possibly then have become compatible with this kind of behaviour (though the mechanisms here are, of course, uncertain) but, Sussman argues, the prime focus lay in the nature of the family economy rather than in attitudes as such.

(vii) THE PRIME MOVERS OF SOCIAL CHANGE

Sussman's discussion raises the more general issue of the role of ideas as causes of social change. Not merely does the sentiments school emphasise the importance of meanings and attitudes surrounding family behaviour but they also see changes in these meanings and attitudes as arising above all as by-products of much more widespread cultural change.

For Shorter, for example, family change is a reflection of the replacement of a traditional 'moral' economy by 'market capitalism'. This new economy opened up communities to wider market and other social influences and exposed consumption and work activities to a *laissez-faire*, individualistically oriented competitive regime. At the same time the proletarianisation of a growing segment of the workforce exposed them to a new set of work relationships. 'The logic of the market place', writes Shorter, 'positively demands individualism' [2:*259*]. Egoism, learnt in the market place, became, he suggests, transferred to community obligations and, above all, to attitudes to familial relationships. A new sexual and emotional 'wish to be free' developed, rooted in these capitalist ideas and this transformed the sexual and familial behaviour of those most affected by the changes, the lower classes.

By contrast, for Stone, the changes in the family between the late sixteenth and late eighteenth centuries are inextricably bound up with changes in religious, philosophical and political thought and also with popular attitudes to the role and rights of individuals in society. Possessive individualism in economic life, a growing emphasis in religious thought on the individualistic nature of the relationship between man and God, and new concepts of the relationship between man and the State had, he suggests, a wider impact on conceptions of appropriate family forms and behaviour. A parallel emphasis on the Enlightenment on the one hand and changing religious doctrine on the other is found in the work of Flandrin, while Trumbach is similarly concerned to stress the importance of a growing egalitarian sentiment [7; 9].

One problem with these mutually contradictory arguments, however intuitively plausible any one or more of them may be, is establishing satisfactorily the actual impact of changes in general philosophical, religious, political or economic ideas on the family behaviour even of the literate minority – let alone of the mass of the population. In none of these cases is this connection clearly documented; indeed, some of the little documentary evidence that is produced is anachronistic in terms of time period and presented without adequate reference to its social, occupational or regional context.

Yet, it remains a crucial issue – and one, indeed, with much wider relevance in social history. Given the available sources the solution is not straightforward. Indeed, probably a total reorientation in research methods is required with a greater stress on how attitudinal change is to be measured and on systematic comparison between different social and regional contexts (or, as in Phayer's work [43], a search for well-documented and fairly short transition points in social ideas which can be linked with reliably measurable indicators of familial change).

But a more general issue also emerges: the role of cultural factors as adequate explanations of familial change. With a few occasional exceptions these authors present a picture of the family's cultural system as detached entirely from the market and work relationships of its members. Family behaviour in the early modern period is seen as held in the grip of traditional, philosophical, religious, community or legal forces. In Stone's, Flandrin's and Ariès's analysis change comes about almost entirely from some combination of a weakening of community and legal constraints and the impact of new religious, philosophical and educational ideas about appropriate relationships between individuals. Change in the economy hardly enters in. Shorter, by contrast, is concerned to stress the impact of capitalism on interpersonal relationships. The main impact, however, is not seen as operating directly to transform relationships between individuals and other members of their families (indeed it cannot be because these relationships have not been analysed in any systematic way for the pre-modern period). Rather the 'ethos of capitalism' (my italics) introduces a wish to be free and 'the ship's own crew – Mom, Dad, and the Kids – ... severed the cables [which tied them to traditional society] by gleefully reaching down and sawing through them so that the solitary voyage could commence' [2:4]. But there is more to capitalism than an ethos; a transformation in economic relationships within the family was involved. Indeed, as the household economy school has shown, capitalism brought with it changes in the whole set of conditions under which 'freedom' (including freedom from other family members) was possible and *allowed* not so much 'Mom, Dad and the Kids' as 'the Kids' to set off alone. By almost ignoring these vital changes in the political economy of the family (indeed by overstressing culture and understressing the underlying factors which make social relationships possible or impossible in any society and to which the culture must relate, and by failing even when they discuss such a relationship to begin to offer a rigorous analysis of it) this group too end up with a partial family history.

It has been a major contribution of the household economics school to begin to draw attention to the role of economic factors in family change. Yet we still lack any really satisfactory account of the relationship between the emergence of ideas like privacy, domesticity and of any change in emotion on the one hand, and the economic transformations of the period 1700 to 1870 on the other.

4 The Household Economics Approach

THIS group of writers has diverse intellectual origins and objectives. What they have in common is their concern with the social processes which underlie family structure (and, though less successfully, familial attitudes) in the past and, in particular, a desire to explore the operation of these processes through their impact on the family as a unit and on relationships between its members. They are thus attempting to tackle the last of what I suggested were the limitations of the demographic approach, the 'family in a thermos flask'. And they are not attempting to solve it, as some demographic workers have, through simply correlating demographic 'facts' with a set of available community-level variables. Instead they start from a quite different methodological position.

This group of writers seeks to interpret households and families above all in the context of the economic behaviour of their members. Of the three groups whose work is reviewed in detail in this pamphlet this group is the most influenced by the methodology (as opposed simply to the techniques) of the social sciences (and particularly of sociology and social anthropology). Thus the questions they raise are inspired not by sources or by observations of the present-day family, but by social-science-inspired theories about the patterning of social relationships and of change in relationships. The main thrust of these theories involves attempts to isolate 'structural' constraints, arising from pressures often quite outside the consciousness of the individuals involved. Central among these factors are those which arise in economic or other exchange relationships within the family and between family members and others. The main emphases are on the ways in which, and the conditions under which, resources (including human resources) become available to the family and to its members, on strategies which can be employed to generate and exploit resources, and on the power relationships which arise as a by-product of these activities. The particular form taken by family behaviour is seen as emerging out of these processes, and the norms, meanings and symbols associated with family behaviour are seen, very largely, not as free-floating independent variables, but as a corollary of these structural constraints.

But how, if those involved are often unaware of their existence, can the operation of these factors be demonstrated? In the work of this school the usual solution has been to use an explicitly comparative methodology. And this group of scholars has pioneered the use of new sources for family history: documents describing property holdings, property utilisation and property transmission, and such material as employment records, family budgets and descriptions of working practices. Even where demographic sources have been used, they have typically been interpreted in the light of evidence of resource generation and consumption activities.

(i) INHERITANCE

A good introduction to the work of this school can be found by looking at recent work on the consequences for family behaviour of different inheritance practices. These practices varied widely across Western societies and even today there are important gaps in our knowledge about the nature and timing of changes in inheritance law in many places. But, for example, in pre-revolutionary France the situation was particularly complicated [Ladurie in 58; 59]. In the south a father could exercise absolute right over the choice of an heir and could transfer most of his property to him, while in much of the north and west he had no power to make any discrimination between his children; even property handed over during his lifetime had to be returned to the common pool for redistribution at his death. In other areas of France a whole range of compromise patterns was found. Elsewhere in Europe, most of the north and west had systems tending to impartibility (land

66

passed to a single heir) but the west of Germany was mostly partible (land divided between children or between sons). Most of the south tended to partibility, but there were many local variations the detail of which is as yet unexplored. And local customs governing actual transmission of land were even more varied than legal patterns and are even less understood. Moreover, for the scholars interested in these problems, wills and property documents are often unreliable guides to the topics of their real interest for they often fail to show property other than land and ignore privileged access to other advantageous rights such as apprenticeship. Also, in law, land rights may have been devolved partibly, whereas in practice siblings frequently gave up their rights in return for a portion to be provided out of the fruits of the estate; conversely, in partible areas, one child might frequently acquire on preferential terms some or all of the land inherited by his siblings.

But why do these differences matter? In his introduction to the most comprehensive collection on this topic the anthropologist Jack Goody argues as follows:

> Transmission *mortis causa* is not only the means by which the reproduction of the social system is carried out . . . ; it is also the way in which interpersonal relationships are structured. I mean by this that since inheritance normally takes place between close kin and affines, the emotional tone and reciprocal rights characterizing such critical relationships are often influenced by the possibility of pooling or dividing the farm or by the anticipation of future gains. . . . Consequently a different quality of relationships, varying family structures, and alternative social arrangements (e.g. greater or lesser migration, age of marriage, rates of illegitimacy) will be linked to differing modes of transmission, whether transmission is primarily lateral or lineal, whether agnatic or uterine, whether to females as well as males, whether equal or unequal [58:*1*].

So, in as far as what is inherited has major importance in the life chances of those receiving it (and this, as we shall see, is an important qualification), the transmission of property not only gives some (but not all) individuals access to resource-generating assets, but also, by the *way* in which it is transmitted and the *point in the life cycle* at which it is transmitted, has potentially much wider ramifications for the structure, demography and quality of family relationships.

A significant body of research is now available in which attempts have been made to link variations and change in family behaviour to both law and practices of property transmission. For example, as we saw in chapter 2, theoretical analysis would suggest that rather more stem-type households would be found in areas with impartible than with partible inheritance, particularly if the property were passed from father to son during the father's lifetime. In the controversial paper described in that chapter this is precisely what Berkner claims to find, with 35 per cent of households in the impartible area being non-nuclear compared with only 13 per cent in the partible area [67]. In his earlier work on Heidenreichstein in Austria, Berkner had also attributed the stem-family pattern to the practice whereby land was transmitted to one heir who used the property both to produce portions for his siblings and to support his father in old age [68]. In France, both Goubert [37] and Flandrin [7] have pointed to the rough geographical association between inheritance practices and household composition, with multi-nuclear households occurring widely in the impartible south and mono-nuclear households widely in the partible north. Flandrin also suggests that the post-1804 laws which enforced partibility on the peasantry brought about a marked fall in complex household forms in the south though the south continued into the nineteenth century to have a larger proportion of non-nuclear households. Moreover, as Flandrin also notes, the fit between inheritance practices and household composition in France is by no means perfect, an observation confirmed by Berkner and Mendels in [18].

Equally ambiguous findings have resulted from attempts to test a model implying more and earlier marriage in partible areas of France by correlating inheritance practices in departments with their age of marriage and proportion of the population married. In part the problem in verifying this kind of proposition statistically arises from difficulties in obtaining adequate indicators: for example, the research just described probably fails in part because the extent of *pre-mortem* transmission of property could not be adequately measured and incorporated into the analysis. But the main problem is that inheritance practices cannot usefully be abstracted from the total set of behaviours which individuals and families employ to sustain and possibly improve their resource-generating capacity, both in the present and into the future; inheritance customs and laws are only one set among a number of interlinked social and economic constraints on family behaviour. In recent years, therefore, the most fruitful insights have come from more comprehensive attempts to analyse and elucidate the consequences for the family of its members' involvement in income-generating processes.

(ii) THE FAMILY ECONOMY OF THE WESTERN PEASANT

This approach has taken as its central concept the often unconscious 'strategies' employed by family members to maintain a customary standard of living, both for themselves in the present and, under certain circumstances, for themselves and their descendants in the future. The types of strategies available are constrained in a number of ways: by the family's resource-generating potential (particularly its age/sex composition); by the mode of production in which the family is involved; by the income-generating relationships which are implied by that mode; by law and custom regarding property acquisition (including inheritance); by the possibilities of access to alternative resource-generating activities (including wage-labour or domestic manufacturing) or resource-providing rights (including, for example, both customary rights to pasture animals on common land and social welfare provision); by the intervention of powerful groups external to the family (landlords, employers and others with power in the local community); by customs limiting the range of resource-generating options which individuals see as practically available at a point in time (for example, ideas over what is appropriate work for women). Useful relevant theoretical discussions are in [72; Elder in 17; Bourdieu in 12; Mendels in *Annales E.S.C.* 1978].

For the Western peasant or yeoman farmer, the principal scarce resource was land, so family strategies were constrained by the conditions under which land could be obtained and by the labour inputs required to work it. The literature on continental Europe, on Ireland, and on some areas of England even in the early nineteenth century, portrays the dominant peasant/yeoman pattern as one where the family's subsistence needs could be met only through the continual application of the labour of all its members to productive tasks in agriculture or, to a greater or lesser extent, in certain craft or other domestically organised productive activities. Almost all production was intended either for family use or for local and known markets.

One of the central problems of the peasant family, from this perspective, was the need to ensure that enough labour was available to meet current and future needs while yet not having too many mouths to feed for the resource-generating capacity of the means of production (for a useful general survey here see Winberg in [14]). On the one hand it was necessary to avoid childless marriages, which gave no security for old age (hence perhaps norms encouraging premarital intercourse to ensure marriage only to fertile girls). On the other hand too many children threatened current subsistence. This problem could, however, in some places be solved by one or more strategic responses. For example: one could acquire more productive resources as children grew (the Russian peasant solution according to Chayanov [69] but not apparently widely used elsewhere); one could expand non-agricultural activities and devote more effort to domestic craft production (but this was not always available) [Löfgren in 14]; one could restrict family size by marriage to older women (certainly used in Norway and Sweden [64; Winberg in 14]), by some form of contraception (found in seventeenth-century England, eighteenth- and early-nineteenth-century Sweden and many other places [26; Gaunt in 15; Winberg in 14; 83]) or by some other strategy such as prolonging breast feeding. Finally, as in England, Scan-

70

dinavia and elsewhere, poor households could regulate their numbers by sending 'surplus' children into service at an early age.

Changes in household composition and differences between regions have similarly been interpreted through relatively simple strategic models. For example the Nivernais in central France in the period from the sixteenth to the nineteenth centuries had a substantial number of multi-nuclear households (particularly those involving co-residing married siblings) and also substantial joint property-holdings between kinsmen. Berkner and Shaffer [70] point to the existence of ancient customary laws assuming or permitting the conscious establishment of 'communities' (persons living in the same household and sharing property and income). Inheritance of property was largely discretionary as long as the father respected certain limited rights of the remaining children, but until the early nineteenth century the conditions under which the land was actually held both prohibited subdivision and required that the heirs be living in common with the deceased at his death; otherwise the land reverted to the lord. This is seen by Berkner and Shaffer as encouraging the formation of joint households in order both to provide for younger siblings and to avoid possible reversion if the heir died childless. From the early seventeenth century onwards, however, land increasingly passed into the lord's hands and was consolidated into substantial farms which were leased to peasants under share-cropping contracts. The traditional joint family did not, however, disappear. Rather the form was adapted to take account of the new conditions and, in particular, to provide the substantial labour force required under conditions where the marginal productivity of labour was too small to allow the employment of servants. The joint family can thus here be seen as a solution – guided by earlier custom and constrained by limitations on partibility – to the problem of efficient exploitation of land resources. Goubert offers a similar explanation for the appearance in the Beauvais and in Poitou in the sixteenth and seventeenth centuries of joint households communally involved in exploiting large consolidated farms [37].

A second example, this time stressing the importance of

non-agricultural by-employments, is described by Gaunt for seventeenth- and eighteenth-century Sweden [61]. Gaunt describes three areas, each of which was part of what he calls a different 'ecotype' in that the household exploited natural resources in ways which involved different work-rhythms over the year and different labour-force requirements. In two of his areas summer agricultural work was complemented by winter employment, in one case in iron mining and manufacturing and in the other in transportation of agricultural and mining products. In the third region there was almost no winter work. Gaunt suggests that a number of major differences in household composition and demographic behaviour can be attributed to these ecotypical differences. In particular, the extra labour requirements and the year-long work-cycle of the two mixed activity areas encouraged the development of larger households, containing more servants and also more relatives. In this case there was also a greater propensity to form stem-type households. A similar point is made for Scandinavia generally by Löfgren [60] who suggests that large complex households typified areas of sparse population with diversified economies; from the eighteenth century the rising population and greater availability of employed labour gradually led to a decline in the 'special economic adaptations' which produced complex families.

It was not, however, only in household composition that Gaunt's areas differed. Fertility was higher in the mixed-economy areas, possibly as a response to greater labour-input needs; but celibacy levels were also markedly higher, probably because in these areas peasants owned their land and there were thus much greater restrictions on the possibilities of marriage. This brings us to another key variable in the models used by scholars of this school: access to resources and its impact on the internal dynamics of household relationships. For the peasant Löfgren specifies the main issues as follows:

> Peasant production was to a great extent based upon a domestic division of labour according to sex and age. This made marriage a necessary condition for a viable farm unit, and the situation of the unmarried peasants

was awkward to say the least. Marriage, though, did not only create a new production unit but also a new unit of capital management, as economic resources like land-holdings, cattle and farm equipment were pooled to make a functional economic cell. The crucial problem therefore was how and on what terms new production units and therefore new marriages were to be set up [60:*30*].

This problem is a complex one; the resources involved were above all land but also equipment, stock, housing and, sometimes vitally, rights to common or to fishing, hunting or gathering [Löfgren in 14; 71]. Over most of Europe (though not always in England [89]) the most normal way in which these resources were acquired was through inheritance or, sometimes, through purchase from one's father as a mechanism of avoiding inheritance laws which would otherwise have led to fragmentation [60]. However, as we have already seen, inheritance laws and customs varied widely between different areas and even between peasants with different kinds and amounts of property; the most general guideline employed was probably flexibility accord-ing to individual circumstances, with the overriding con-sideration even in impartible areas being to provide some future for as many children as possible, rather than simply providing the best possible future for one.

But, no matter which system was in operation, as long as parents remained the main source of acquiring the means of production and as long as they had discretion over how it was distributed between children, the internal dynamics of family life were crucially influenced by when and how they exercised their discretion [63; 60]. On the one hand parents had immense potential control over whom their children could marry and when (a control, of course, exercised even more strongly, but for the same reasons, by the landowning élites). But (and here there is an important difference from the élites) this control was mitigated by the need for the father and mother to secure their own old age; to do this they generally needed to make provision for at least one of their children within their own lifetimes, their position normally being secured by a legally valid contract which

73

prevented the child from breaking his side of the bargain. Moreover, non-inheriting children had a motive to co-operate since they would in this way be improving the capital out of which their own provision would be obtained. So we can best conceptualise these peasant households as involving *mutual interdependence* but with possibilities for considerable conflict and mistrust both between and within generations.

However, this situation would presumably vary according to the extent of parental discretion on the one hand and the availability to children of alternative means of production on the other. The first possibility has not been fully explored (but see [7; 60]) but the second corresponds with the findings of a number of studies. For example larger farmers who could offer larger inheritances were usually more successful at retaining children at home to support them in old age than were small farmers [75; 60; 43]; in late eighteenth- and early nineteenth-century Ireland there is some evidence that the availability of waste land and of emigration, together with the possibility raised by the potato of subsistence on smaller parcels of land, encouraged a shift towards subdivision of holdings and earlier marriage [63]; the arrival of by-employment had a similar effect [Braun in 18 – see below]. In colonial North America the availability of new land to the West seems to have freed the settlers from many of the constraints of European farming life thus encouraging both earlier marriage and higher fertility as well as a greater independence from parental control [Withey in *J. Fam. Hist.* 1978; 65]. Finally, the availability of agricultural resources in England through an extensive market in land seems possibly to have been of key importance in producing the rather different familial practices of that country, involving as they did children even in prosperous families leaving home at an early age to go into service and subsequently acquiring farms on their own account [89]. Interpretation of change in England is, however, difficult because of the early impact of the proletarianisation of labour.

(iii) THE PROLETARIANISATION OF LABOUR

The previous section outlined a pattern of Western family life the salient features of which remain largely unchanged even today in many of the more remote peasant areas of Europe. The same basic structural conditions (and presumably the same basic family patterns though the topic is much under-researched) have applied also to those artisans like village bakers who continued with a family-based production system involving their own skill and capital and producing only for the needs of a known local market. But long before the arrival of factories, indeed certainly in substantial numbers from the seventeenth century (and earlier in England) two other groups became increasingly important in the Western economy: landless labourers (or cottagers with inadequate land or with no control over who was to succeed them) and proto-industrial workers.

For the landless labourer, the structural conditions under which subsistence-generating activities took place were quite different from those of the peasant [compare Löfgren in 14]. Whereas the peasant household served as the centre of economic activity in which the older generation co-ordinated and directed the work of the younger in a joint process of production, for the agricultural labourer the productive activities of at least some family members were directed and co-ordinated by outsiders in the interests not of the family but of themselves, and in ways which frequently conflicted with the interests of the labourers' families as a whole. Of course, some production functions remained, at least until the extinction of customary rights of gathering wild food and firing, of gleaning and pasture, and until the reduction in size of gardens in which significant quantities of food could be raised; Löfgren in particular is concerned to demonstrate the integrated, interdependent and flexible strategies, involving all resident and many absent family members which were adopted by landless labourers to cope with these situations of economic marginality. In other areas family members were sent or moved away for a time (harvest migrants from Ireland, temporary out-migrants from highland Switzerland, children of poor labourers sent into service [63; Braun in 18; 38]) as part of a similar strategy. Nevertheless, in general the standard of living of labouring families was much more dependent on means of production which they did not control. This both made them less secure in the short run (particularly where there was a seasonal demand for labour) and had implications for their support in old age when incomes were likely to fall but no means remained to induce support from their children (who anyway were usually unable to help because of their own economic marginality). The consequences for kinship relations were thus very different from those of the peasant [Löfgren in 14; 85; see also 73].

Presumably one would also expect a second set of differences between agricultural labourers and peasant producers which would serve to exacerbate the problems of the aged. If marriage age and fertility among peasants are constrained by the need to wait until income-generating resources have been acquired by inheritance and by the need to restrict the numbers of children for whom provision has to be made in the next generation, then the absence of anything to be distributed to the next generation should remove these constraints; indeed since maximum earning capacity came while one was young, quite the opposite pressures can be posited. These predictions fit nicely with Levine's findings [74] – though based on rather thin data – both of early marriage and high fertility in proletarianised villages and of changes in this direction during proletarianisation of agricultural labour at periods when local élite groups were unable to constrain marriage [see also Löfgren in 14; 44; 43; but see the opposite trend described in 83].

Similar structural changes in the direction of proletarianisation were also going forward with increasing rapidity between the seventeenth and the early nineteenth centuries among that section of the rural population who were becoming involved in forms of artisan production (especially in textiles, but also in furniture, metal-working, clothing and many other areas) which were increasingly oriented to distant anonymous mass markets serviced through and subject to the control of putters-out. Superficially, perhaps, this form of production appears to be little different from the peasant farm or from more traditional locally oriented artisan production. There were, however, two differences. Firstly, because production was aimed at an increasingly unstable capitalist market the returns for labour varied dramatically from year to year, this insecurity being exacerbated by attempts by putters-out to have available enough labour to meet maximum demand. More importantly, certain basic processes operated quite differently in these families, with important consequences for the strategies adopted by their members. Crucially, the 'foundation and continuing existence of the family as a unit of production and consumption was no longer necessarily tied to the transmission of property through inheritance. It was replaced by the possibility of founding a family primarily as a unit of labour' [73:*303*]. This possibility was furthered where, as increasingly happened, the putter-out not only provided the raw materials and specified the designs (thus removing most of the need for working capital and craft traditions) but also owned the fixed capital in the form of machinery (stocking frame, loom, and so on) and even (for example in handloom 'factories') working space. Freed from the constraints over marriage, individuals with no dowry or inheritance could nevertheless establish themselves in independent households at an early age; indeed there were incentives to do so both to raise their standard of living and to have children while their productive capacity was high.

It is to these factors that scholars have attributed a fall in the age of marriage and the rises in fertility which often follow proto-industrialisation [for example 74], with desperate attempts to reduce family size following when conditions subsequently worsened; perhaps even infanticide and child abandonment are best seen within this framework, as well as high illegitimacy in bad years. Two other effects have also been suggested. Firstly, Braun [in 18; 78], writing on eighteenth-century Switzerland stresses the looseness of relationships between parents and children which were frequently commented on by contemporaries and which have also been observed in some early factory towns [75]. Secondly, Levine [74] points to the 'huddling' of relatives together in large complex households (particularly in the most poverty-stricken stages of the

77

family life cycle) and sees this as a reaction to the increasing pressure on the household economy in the dying phases of framework knitting; the end result of this process was often to produce multi-nuclear households with a structure similar to peasant stem families, but both Levine and Medick [73] are concerned to stress that the strategies involved in reaching this form are quite different.

It is worth stressing that none of the effects described in the last few paragraphs involved what have traditionally been seen as the main elements in social change in the 'Industrial Revolution'. None of the workers so far described worked in factories, none necessarily lived in urban areas and none had been involved in migrations any more substantial than those which had typified earlier social forms. The crucial variables were rather the freeing of individuals' life chances from parental control and the consequent declining interdependence between generations. So what, if anything, was uniquely new about the industrialisation and mass migrations of the nineteenth century as far as their effects on the family are concerned?

Far from the almost universal picture of disorganisation and disruption of family relationships perceived by many contemporaries and earlier scholars, recent work has stressed the extent to which 'traditional' attitudes influenced the strategies adopted by families whose members became involved in factory and other large-scale capitalist work organisation. The strategies adopted are also seen as primarily operating at the familial and household rather than the individual level [see especially 72]. However, the relationship is not seen only as a one-way affair; the same research also stresses the need for employers to adopt strategies of labour recruitment which did not interfere too drastically with these same 'traditional' value systems. Seen in this light, optimal outcomes were different among sections of the proletariat from different economic and cultural backgrounds, in different industries, in different countries, and at different times; so research has increasingly begun to focus on diversity of actions and reactions rather than on any single set of effects, and to emphasise the continuities – and even in some cases the strengthening of family bonds – brought about by industrialisation and mass migration.

The continuities were many (there is a good review in [80]). Much factory industrialisation took place in small village communities, and even where towns were involved only a minority of the adult employed population was usually engaged in factory work. Factories took men and women out of the home but agricultural labourers, masons, carters and many others had traditionally worked away from home, sometimes for long periods. In many areas women had worked in the fields taking their children with them and, until it was suppressed by law, they continued to do so in many early factories. In fact, few married women worked in factories and only tiny numbers of women with small children did so, in contrast to the impression given by much misinformed contemporary as well as more recent historical comment. Instead, most remained in the vital and even expanding domestic occupations such as clothing and food production – and by doing so made significant contributions to the family economy.

Moreover, most of the urban factory labour force did not consist of young men and women of peasant stock who had come alone to live in lodgings in a large city cut off from friends and relatives, working in a huge factory as part of an atomised labour force. Instead, more often than not, migration and entry to factory employment were acts pursued within a family-oriented social context; most migration was highly focused onto particular places (and jobs within places) where the opportunities available to the migrant would match if possible the skills and earning potential of himself and his family and would be set within a context which would not conflict with values brought from the sending community.

For example, in Lancashire many urban textile factory workers seem to have had some experience in rural textile industries, while girls from peasant farming backgrounds followed traditional patterns by going mainly into domestic service [75]. Where they did not, as in some areas of France and Italy [80], some employers set up factory dormitories, supervised by nuns who acted as substitute parents (compare, though without the nuns, Dubnoff in *J. Fam. Hist.* 1979 for the United States); in this way the girls' parents

79

would have been somewhat reassured that the new employers differed only minimally in their paternalistic care for their daughters (and particularly for their morals) from the masters to whom their daughters would otherwise have been sent as servants. Similarly, research on many areas of Europe in the nineteenth century and in North America up to the inter-war period has shown that most migration was not undertaken by atomised individuals knowing nothing about where they were going or why. Rather, migrants moved, probably a majority in family groups, along networks of relatives and friends, often at the instigation of these relatives and friends, to temporary homes provided by them and to jobs obtained with their assistance – indeed, often, under the formal or informal subcontracting systems common in industry up to the First World War, to jobs under their direct control [for example 81]. The timing and direction of migration would often have been decided for family reasons – young men and women sent away from home to remit their surplus earnings to support their younger siblings at home or to save for their own marriages back in the rural community. For the landless labourer or the poor widow, however, there was an alternative: to take advantage of the high wages paid to small children in some industrial areas and to move the whole family in order to maximise familial income even if, as sometimes happened, this led to a fall in the wages of the adult male, or even to his total unemployment, or to his becoming the chief domestic worker in the family. This situation, which was so much deplored by contemporaries, can be seen from a household economics perspective as a perfectly rational strategy and one, incidentally, which kept together a family which would otherwise have been split up (for a useful summary discussion here see [80]). And taking in relatives or lodgers can be seen as another strategy, used to raise the income of certain groups at certain points in the life cycle [81; 75].

The pattern, then, involved an immensely flexible response to new situations and numerous continuities for many of those involved; but it also involved subtle differences between groups and industries, only a few of which have so far been fully explored. One crucial set of differences were the employment opportunities available to

80

married women and children and the different ways in which these groups could contribute to the family economy (usefully discussed by McLaughlin in [11]; also in [72]). In part these differences between groups relate to what kind of work it was seen as proper for women to do and how much the work interfered with their ability to look after small children. But it also related to what was available; for example, textile areas, which were almost unique in early industrialisation in offering factory employment to women and children of both sexes, seem to have had distinctive patterns of kinship behaviour (aged parents being used to care for house and young children while mother worked in the mill [75]) and possibly of conjugal relationships as well. The same was true of fertility, women in textile areas seeking to restrict fertility so as not to interfere with their work (compare also artisan silk weavers in Lyons [82]). In all respects they differed from mining areas where, as was increasingly the case elsewhere, there was only domestic work for women and where there was no role for the aged: the optimal strategy here was to have as many boys as soon as possible so that they could contribute to family income [Tilly in 16].

So recent work in this tradition stresses cohesion, adaptability and continuity and an interdependent household economy often involving consciously worked-out strategies of moving family members in and out of different areas of industry (even into areas where children's wages were high but adult wages low with deleterious effects on their future life chances [Shaffer in *J. Fam. Hist.* 1978]), while incorporating different combinations of outsiders (kin, lodgers or both at different points in the life cycle) in order to attain a target income, and also attempting to make adequate provision for meeting domestic needs. In turn these strategies had implications for a range of demographic and familial behaviour. Sometimes the best strategy was to buy rather than make food and clothing, again something which shocked incomprehending middle-class contemporaries. Interdependence is seen as sometimes extending to relatives outside the conjugal family, encouraging them to live near and with each other as a means of securing more congenial housing and better jobs, an insurance, however

81

meagre, against inevitable and frequent crises such as sickness, injury, and unemployment, against which no other adequate provision existed [75].

Yet there is a danger in the work of this school of over-romanticising the picture by exaggerating continuity and cohesion, just as earlier writing exaggerated disruption. In part it is a problem of evidence – one knows when one finds evidence of cohesive behaviour but when one does not it is unclear whether there is simply no evidence or whether behaviour was in fact different. There certainly is some evidence that all strategies were not equally effective in the long run [Elder in 17], of individuals lonely and starving, of women forced to adopt solutions involving prostitution in order to keep themselves and their children alive, of contemporary descriptions of children leaving home to set up in lodgings so as not to have to live in poor overcrowded households [75], and of material which would support statements such as that of the journalist, who in 1849 likened Lancashire family behaviour to that of members of a joint stock company where

> as surely as the different personages of the company begin to perceive that they are contributing either in money or in comfort of situation more to the family than the family contributes to them, so surely they withdraw from the association to labour in isolation or to form new and more profitable social combinations for themselves [*Morning Chronicle Supplement*, 1 January 1850].

And part of this change clearly reflects the fact that, while in the short run children's optimal individual strategies typically involved co-operation in conjugal family income-generating activities, in the long run their own interests lay – as they had in the proto-industrial economy – not in succeeding to a familial enterprise or in deriving income-generating resources from it but in establishing their own households, often in new places and based on their own individual labour [75; 43; 66]. This difference is clearly reflected in the experience of Polish migrants to the United States in the early twentieth century when family-based strategies, involving sending money back home, rapidly became undermined by individualistic strategies emphasising the right of the individual to keep wages for his or her own future purposes ([79]; note also the more theoretical discussion of situations of breakdown or non-establishment of kin-based relationships in Smelser in [19]).

Indeed much familial behaviour among urban industrial workers can be seen from a rather different perspective as a more direct result of the conceptions of the individual and family which characterised Western capitalism. For example, the capitalist practice of paying wages to an individual and defining this wage as the individual's own property rather than as a reward received on behalf of the family was reflected in a more egocentric attitude to a man's wage, and provided rationale for some men to spend a significant proportion of it on drink, much to the despair of their wives and to the shock of middle-class contemporaries. Individual wages can also be seen as supporting the devaluation of housework to a status where, because it was not paid, it was also not 'really' work. Similarly the fact that the man was defined as the family wage-earner also legitimised irregular employment and below-subsistence wages for women's home work (regardless of the fact that many single-parent families had to rely solely on them [Shaffer in *J. Fam. Hist.* 1978]). And the middle-class image of the family can be seen as finally winning out, with the extension of compulsory education and child-labour legislation in the later years of the nineteenth and in the twentieth century; the consequence was that children's ability to contribute to the family economy became increasingly undermined and the whole basis of interdependence between generations disappeared [88; 84]. We are moving here beyond a purely household-economics perspective towards some preliminary attempts to suggest how wider structural forces operated on the family. But a problem immediately arises; it is one thing to propose plausible structurally-based transformations and quite another to document their precise impact on family attitudes and behaviour and to rule out alternative cultural interpretations such as might be made by some sentiments writers.

And more generally the household economics perspective is no panacea; compared with the demographic approach, the theoretical requirement on the household economics school to focus on detailed comparisons of processes as they affected limited groups of the population tends to lead to partial accounts which ignore the experiences of large sections of the population for whom the particular structural changes under discussion were irrelevant. In some ways this kind of social history replaces older historians' accounts of the behaviour of élites by accounts confined to different minorities involved in theoretically interesting structural transformations. Equally, changes in attitudes can never be understood simply as a reflection of structural changes.

So just as a demographic approach is inadequate if it fails to take account of meaning and of the relationships between family behaviour and the wider economy and society, and just as a sentiments approach is incomplete if it ignores behaviour and the economic and social context which constrains the ideas it describes, so the sentiments and demographic approaches complement the more structural approach of the household economics school. We must therefore expect the three very different lines of approach to continue to be followed in family history, as, indeed, they have been in other areas of social history and in social science more generally.

Select Bibliography

This list of works is intended to provide a basic introduction to the literature (particularly the literature in English) on the history of the white Western family for the period covered by the pamphlet; it is in no way an exhaustive list of sources used in preparing the work. The place of publication is London unless otherwise stated.

The *Journal of Family History* [*J. Fam. Hist.*] has rapidly established itself as the principal specialist journal in the field and it will provide the best source for updating this bibliography in the coming years.

GENERAL SURVEY WORKS

[1]   T. P. R. Laslett, *Family Life and Illicit Love in Earlier Generations* (1977). A collection of papers showing Laslett's more recent work. The introduction is a clear statement of his position on family history.

[2]   E. Shorter, *The Making of the Modern Family* (1976). An immensely stimulating book marred by a distracting style, some grossly inflated generalisation on the basis of minimal data (sometimes used out of context) and an over-emphasis on vaguely conceptualised cultural causation.

[3]   R. T. Vann, Review of [2], *J. Fam. Hist.*, I (1976). A scholarly review.

[4]   L. Stone, *The Family, Sex and Marriage in England, 1500–1800* (1977). An impressive attempt at an impossible task; valuable on the upper classes and almost useless on the rest of society.

[5]   A. Macfarlane, Review of [4], *History and Theory*, XVIII (1979).

[6] E. P. Thompson, Review of [4], *New Society* (8 September 1977).
[5] and [6] are two very different, useful reviews.

[7] J. L. Flandrin, *Families in Former Times* (1979). A fragmented book which nevertheless provides invaluable insights and material on France and England, by France's currently foremost family historian.

[8] P. Ariès, *Centuries of Childhood* (1972). A seminal work on more than just children which inspired a whole new approach to family history.

[9] R. Trumbach, *The Rise of the Egalitarian Family; Aristocratic Kinship and Domestic Relations in Eighteenth Century England* (1978).

[10] M. Mitteraur and R. Sieder, *The European Family* (1982). An interesting survey.

COLLECTIONS OF PAPERS

[11] T. K. Rabb and R. I. Rotberg (eds), *The Family in History* (1973). A very useful collection. The papers by Goubert, Shorter, Wells and McLaughlin are all valuable.

[12] R. Forster and O. Ranum (eds), *Family and Society* (1976). A useful collection of French work, translated from *Annales E. S. C.*

[13] W. Conze (ed.), *Sozialgeschichte der Familie in der Neuzeit Europas: neue Forschungen* (Stuttgart 1976). Includes a number of valuable pieces not available elsewhere.

[14] S. Åkerman *et al.* (ed.), *Chance and Change* (Odense 1978). A useful collection of Scandinavian papers on family and demographic history.

[15] S. Åkerman *et al.* (ed.), *Aristocrats, Farmers and Proletarians: Essays in Swedish Demographic History* (Uppsala 1973). An earlier collection, more demographic in content.

[16] J. Sundin *et al.* (ed.), *Time, Space and Man* (Uppsala

1979). The papers of a microdemography seminar held in Umeå, Sweden.

[17] T. K. Hareven (ed.), *Transitions: the Family and the Life Course in Historical Perspective* (1978). A series of papers stressing the importance of the inter-relations between family life cycle, individual life course and historical time.

[18] C. Tilly (ed.), *Historical Studies of Changing Fertility* (Princeton 1978). Covers more than just fertility; Tilly's introduction is a useful review of recent work in historical demography.

[19] J. Demos and S. S. Bocock (eds), *Turning Points: Historical and Sociological Essays on the Family* (Supplement to *American Journal of Sociology* 1978). Shows well the major recent American trends in research; combines some useful historical case studies with some perceptive sociological commentary.

[20] K. W. Wachter *et al.*, *Statistical Studies of Historical Social Structure* (1978). A pioneering book on simulation in family history; mainly on household composition.

THE DEMOGRAPHIC CONTEXT

[21] M. W. Flinn, *British Population Growth 1700–1850* (1970).

[22] R. M. Mitchison, *British Population Change since 1860* (1977).

[23] E. A. Wrigley and R. Schofield, *The Population History of England 1541–1871* (forthcoming).

[24] A. J. Coale, 'The Decline of Fertility in Europe from the French Revolution to World War II', in S. J. Behrman (ed.), *Fertility and Family Planning* (Ann Arbor 1969).
[21] to [24] are four useful surveys of demographic trends and interpretations.

[25] L. Henry, *Anciennes Familles Genevoises* (Paris 1956).

[26] E. A. Wrigley, 'Family Limitation in Pre-Industrial England', *Economic History Review*, XIX (1966).
[25] and [26] clearly demonstrate family limitation before the nineteenth century.

[27]   J. A. Banks, *Prosperity and Parenthood: A Study of Family Planning among the Victorian Middle Class* (1954).
[28]   D. S. Smith, 'A Homeostatic Demographic Regime: Patterns in West European Family Reconstitution Studies', in R. D. Lee (ed.), *Population Patterns in the Past* (1977).
[29]   K. Gaskin, 'Age at First Marriage in Europe before 1850', *J. Fam. Hist.*, III (1978).
       [28] and [29] are two useful recent attempts to summarise findings from family reconstitution studies.
[30]   R. M. Smith, 'Population and its Geography in England 1500–1730', in R. Butlin and R. Dodgshon (eds), *An Historical Geography of England and Wales* (1978).
[31]   J. Hajnal, 'European Marriage Patterns in Perspective', in D. V. Glass and D. E. C. Eversley (eds), *Population in History* (1965). A pioneering survey.

THE FAMILY LIFE CYCLE

(see also Le Bras and Wachter in [20]; Wells in [11]; [17]).
[32]   J. Fourastié, 'From the Traditional to the "Tertiary" Life Cycle', in W. Petersen (ed.), *Readings in Population* (1972).
[33]   P. C. Glick and R. Parke, 'New Approaches in Studying the Life Cycle of the Family', *Demography*, II (1965).

HOUSEHOLD COMPOSITION

(see also [74])
[34]   T. P. R. Laslett (ed.), *Household and Family in Past Time* (1972). The collection of papers which established the systematic analysis of household composition. Shows well the strengths and weaknesses of Laslett's approach.
[35]   L. K. Berkner, 'The Use and Misuse of Census Data for the Historical Analysis of Family Structure', *Journal of Interdisciplinary History*, V (1975). A critical review of [34].

[36] L. K. Berkner, 'Rural Family Organization in Europe: a Problem in Comparative History', *Peasant Studies Newsletter*, I (1972). Particularly useful on conceptual points.

[37] P. Goubert, 'Family and Province: A Contribution to the Knowledge of Family Structures in Early Modern France', *J: Fam. Hist.*, II (1977). A scathing attack on Laslett, with some useful if impressionistic French material.

[38] R. Wall , 'The Age at Leaving Home', *J. Fam. Hist.*, III (1978).

[39] J. Modell and T. K. Hareven, 'Urbanization and the Malleable Household: An Examination of Boarding and Lodging in American Families', *Journal of Marriage and the Family*, XXXV (1973).

ILLEGITIMACY AND PREMARITAL CONCEPTION

(see also [1]; [2]; Shorter in [11]).

[40] T. P. R. Laslett *et al.*, *Bastardy and its Comparative History* (1980). An important if long-delayed collection of papers on various countries.

[41] J. Knodel *et al.*, 'The Decline of Non-marital Fertility in Europe 1880–1941', *Population Studies*, XXV (1971). A comprehensive review suggesting contraception as crucial.

[42] L. A. Tilly *et al.*, 'Women's Work and European Fertility Patterns', *Journal of Interdisciplinary History*, VI (1976). An interesting attack on Shorter.

[43] J. M. Phayer, *Sexual Liberation and Religion in Nineteenth Century Europe* (1977). Pretentiously titled, being based only on limited areas of France and Germany, but useful and fairly persuasive on them.

[44] J. Frykman, 'Sexual Intercourse and Social Norms: A Study of Illegitimate Births in Sweden 1831–1939', *Ethnologia Scandinavica*, III (1975). Useful; the argument has wider relevance.

[45] D. S. Smith and M. S. Hindus, 'Premarital Pregnancy in America 1640–1971: An Overview and Interpretation', *Journal of Interdisciplinary History*, V (1975).

[46]   T. C. Smout, 'Aspects of Sexual Behaviour in Nineteenth Century Scotland', in A. A. MacLaren (ed.),
Social Class in Scotland: Past and Present (Edinburgh
1976).
[47]   I. Carter, 'Illegitimate Births and Illegitimate Inferences', *Scottish Journal of Sociology*, I (1977).
[48]   T. C. Smout, 'Illegitimacy: a Reply', *Scottish Journal of
Sociology*, II (1977).
[46] to [48] are of substantive interest, but the dispute
over method and interpretation is particularly valuable.

MARRIAGE

(see also [4]; [31]).
[49]   P. D. Hall, 'Marital Selection and Business in
Massachusetts Merchant Families 1700–1900', in R.
L. Coser (ed.), *The Family: its Structures and Functions*
(1974).
[50]   D. Crozier, 'Kinship and Occupational Succession',
Sociological Review, new series, XIII (1965).
[51]   L. Davidoff, *The Best Circles: Society, Etiquette and the
Season* (1973). Valuable on upper-class courtship
institutions.

PRIVACY AND DOMESTICITY

(see also [2]; [4]; [7]).
[52]   B. Laslett, 'The Family as a Public and Private
Institution: a Historical Perspective', *Journal of Marriage and the Family*, XXXV (1973).
[53]   C. E. Clark, 'Domestic Architecture as an Index to
Social History: The Romantic Revival and the Cult of
Domesticity in America 1840–1870', *Journal of Interdisciplinary History*, VII (1976).

CHILDREN IN THE FAMILY

(see also [2]; [8]).
[54]   L. de Mauṣe (ed.), *The History of Childhood* (New York
1974). The manifesto of the psychohistory school; de

Mause's introduction shows the limitations and one or two papers some strengths.

[55] I. Pinchbeck and M. Hewitt, *Children in English Society*, 2 vols (1969). An invaluable survey, though better on evidence of behaviour than interpretation.

[56] G. D. Sussman, 'The End of the Wet-Nursing Business in France 1874–1914', *J. Fam. Hist.*, II (1977). An attack on Shorter but of wider relevance.

[57] P. Greven, *The Protestant Temperament: Patterns of Child-Rearing, Religious Experience and the Self in Early America* (New York 1977). Important for its emphasis on diversity in the same country at the same time.

INHERITANCE AND THE FAMILY

[58] J. Goody *et al.* (eds), *Family and Inheritance: Rural Society in Western Europe 1200–1800* (1976). An influential collection of papers with a perceptive theoretical introduction by Goody.

[59] A. I. Hermalin and E. van de Walle, 'The Civil Code and Nuptiality', in R. D. Lee (ed.), *Population Patterns in the Past* (1977). They qualify Ladurie's picture in [58].

PEASANT FAMILIES

[60] O. Löfgren, 'Family and Household among Scandinavian Peasants', *Ethnologia Scandinavia*, II (1974). Very valuable, with implications far outside Scandinavia.

[61] D. Gaunt, 'Preindustrial Economy and Population Structure', *Scandinavian Journal of History*, II (1977). Valuable for its material on ecotypically based variations.

[62] C. M. Arensberg and S. T. Kimball, *Family and Community in Ireland* (1940). On Ireland in the 1930s, but a classic peasant study.

[63] K. H. Connell, *Irish Peasant Society: Four Historical Essays* (Oxford 1968).

[64] M. Drake, *Population and Society in Norway 1735–1865* (1969).

[65] P. J. Greven, *Four Generations: Population, Land and*

Family in Colonial Andover, Massachusetts (Ithaca 1970). A pioneering local study and still one of the best.

[66]   J. Demos, *A Little Commonwealth: Family Life in Plymouth Colony* (1970). Another valuable pioneering work.

[67]   L. K. Berkner, 'Peasant Household Organisation and Demographic Change in Lower Saxony (1689–1766)', in R. D. Lee (ed.), *Population Patterns in the Past* (1977).

[68]   L. K. Berkner, 'The Stem Family and the Developmental Cycle of the Peasant Household: an Eighteenth Century Austrian Example', *American Historical Review*, ɪxxv (1972). A perceptive early study of life cycle and family economy.

[69]   A. V. Chayanov, *The Theory of Peasant Economy* (Homewood, Illinois 1966). A classic study of the Russian peasantry but of doubtful applicability elsewhere.

[70]   L. K. Berkner and J. W. Shaffer, 'The Joint Family in the Nivernais', *J. Fam. Hist.*, ɪɪɪ (1978). A good case study.

[71]   M. Spufford, *Contrasting Communities: English Villages in the Sixteenth and Seventeenth Centuries* (1974). Some excellent case studies; particularly strong on how inheritance worked in practice.

PROTO-INDUSTRIALISATION, PROLETARIANISATION AND URBAN-INDUSTRIAL FAMILY LIFE

[72]   L. A. Tilly, 'Individual Lives and Family Strategies in the French Proletariat', *J. Fam. Hist.*, ɪv (1979). A clear and coherent statement and example of the use of the concept of 'strategies' for family analysis.

[73]   H. Medick, 'The Proto-industrial Family Economy: the Structural Function of Household and Family during the Transition from Peasant to Industrial Capitalism', *Social History*, ɪ (1976). A seminal paper in every way.

[74]   D. Levine, *Family Formation in an Age of Nascent Capitalism* (1977). The first British community

monograph to link demography with economic and social change. Valuable, though at times the interpretations outrun the data.

[75] M. Anderson, *Family Structure in Nineteenth Century Lancashire* (1971). Particularly concerned with the impact of industrialisation and migration on kinship behaviour.

[76] M. Katz, *The People of Hamilton, Canada West: Family and Class in a Mid-Nineteenth Century City* (Cambridge, Mass., 1975). Naive in its discussion of meaning, but containing useful material on household membership over time.

[77] R. Sennett, *Families against the City: Middle Class Homes of Industrial Chicago* (Harvard 1970). Thought-provoking, though some of the inferences seem rather shaky.

[78] R. Braun, *Industrialisierung und Volksleben* (Winterthur 1960). A classic study; there is a summary of some of the material in [18].

[79] W. I. Thomas and F. Znaniecki, *The Polish Peasant in Europe and America* (New York 1919–20). A classic still worth study.

[80] J. Scott and L. Tilly, 'Women's Work and the Family in Nineteenth Century Europe', *Comparative Studies in Society and History*, XVII (1975). A seminal work pioneering the modern use of the concept of family economy.

[81] T. K. Hareven, 'Family Time and Industrial Time: Family and Work in a Planned Corporation Town 1900–1924', *Journal of Urban History*, I (1975).

[82] L. S. Strumingher, 'The Artisan Family: Traditions and Transition in Nineteenth Century Lyons', *J. Fam. Hist.*, II (1977).

[83] I. Eriksson and J. Rogers, *Rural Labor and Population Change: Social and Demographic Developments in East-central Sweden during the Nineteenth Century* (Uppsala 1978).

MISCELLANEOUS

[84] M. Anderson, 'The Relevance of Family History', in

C. C. Harris (ed.), *The Sociology of the Family: Contemporary Developments* (Keele 1980). An attempt at a long-run view.

[85]   M. Anderson, 'The Impact on the Family Relationships of the Elderly of Changes since Victorian Times in Governmental Income-Maintenance Provision', in E. Shanas and M. B. Sussman (eds), *Family, Bureaucracy and the Elderly* (Durham, N. C. 1977).

[86]   J. R. Gillis, *Youth and History: Tradition and Change in European Age Relations 1770 – Present* (1974).

[87]   B. Hanssen, 'Dimensions of Primary Group Structure in Sweden', in UNESCO *Recherches sur la Famille*, vol. 1 (Tübingen 1956). A.clear expression of Hanssen's views in English.

[88]   C. Lasch, *Haven in a Heartless World* (1977).
The early chapters are useful on the 'professionalisation' of parenthood and provocative on the causes.

[89]   A. Macfarlane, *The Origins of English Individualism: the Family, Property and Social Transition* (Oxford 1978).
A provocative work which argues that England has not been a peasant society since the early Middle Ages; while making an important point it exaggerates it by over-emphasising the importance of law and setting up a theoretical conception of 'peasant' which leads the analysis to a foregone conclusion.

[90]   R. M. Titmuss, *Essays on the Welfare State* (1958).

Index

95